Stuff Happens!

Manage your clutter, clear your head & discover what's really important

Emma Gleeson

SANDYCOVE

an imprint of

PENGUIN BOOKS

SANDYCOVE

UK | USA | Canada | Ireland | Australia
India | New Zealand | South Africa

Sandycove is part of the Penguin Random House group of companies
whose addresses can be found at global.penguinrandomhouse.com

First published 2021
001

Copyright © Emma Gleeson, 2021

The moral right of the author has been asserted

Set in 12.5/14.75pt Garamond MT Std
Typeset by Jouve (UK), Milton Keynes
Printed and bound in Great Britain by Clays Ltd, Elcograf S.p.A.

The authorized representative in the EEA is Penguin Random House Ireland,
Morrison Chambers, 32 Nassau Street, Dublin D02 YH68

A CIP catalogue record for this book is available from the British Library

ISBN: 978–1–844–88489–6

www.greenpenguin.co.uk

For Michael and Joan

Contents

CONTENTS

PART 4
Organization

PART 5
Our Broken Relationship with Stuff

PART 6
Changing Your Ways for Good

Introduction

This book is about getting to grips with your stuff in the midst of a busy life. It is not just about tidying your house. Many versions of that book already exist. It is a look under the bonnet of our shopping habits, which are the main root causes of household clutter. Clutter is the symptom, but the way we value our possessions is the problem, from the moment we buy them to when it's time to let them go.

While some of us are naturally better than others at avoiding its clutches, clutter is an increasingly troublesome by-product of the way those of us who live in wealthy countries operate. Clutter affects all of us in different ways. Some people are experts at hiding it from sight and others manage to clear it out quickly (often only to make room for more). Some people don't give a damn about the clutter in their homes and live their lives in their own brand of perfectly organized chaos. Then there is another type of person, one who feels suffocated by a house full of stuff but can never find the bloody hammer, or Sellotape, or a particular dress when they need it. No matter what kind of person you are, there will be something in these pages for you.

It's up to you how you use this book. You might prefer

to skip the sections that look at the psychology of shopping and only read the 'how-to-declutter-your-home' chapters. I would gently advise against this. It would be like someone going to psychotherapy for the first time and saying to the therapist, 'I know I have issues, but no childhood stuff, please.'

Here's the truth: Decluttering our homes without looking at why we have so much stuff in the first place is like going on a crash diet – it won't stick and you'll be back to square one within months.

We need to properly understand why we feel so compelled to accumulate possessions. We need to recognize that this acquisitive way of life does not make us happy. We need to care about where our possessions come from, how they are made, and by whom. From there, real change can begin to take place.

For many years now, I have helped people declutter their homes and organize their possessions. I am admittedly one of those weirdos who gets a kick out of decluttering. Some people relax by ironing; a high-powered executive I know unwinds by polishing silver – it takes all sorts. My particular quirk means that I have come to care deeply about our relationships with the things that aid and decorate our lives. I also have an MA in Fashion History and have been fascinated by material culture and the stories behind everyday objects for the past decade.

My aim with this book is not to preach. Decluttering and organizing has become another means of making people (well, let's be honest – women) feel like they are not doing enough. All too often it is just another Keeping up with the Joneses competition. I want to strip all that away and offer a more measured view of the benefits of decluttering our lives, such as the feeling of lightness when the burden of stuff is lifted, a renewed sense of gratitude for all that you have, and a shift towards more mindful shopping and disposal habits.

Here's my decluttering philosophy in a nutshell:

- Let your home only contain items that you use and that you love.*
- Store your possessions in a way that makes sense for you.
- Pass items on responsibly when you are finished with them.
- Pay more attention to how and why new items enter your home in the first place.

It has taken me many years of discovery to reach this perspective. I used to be someone who collected scraps of fabric and paper, unwearable charity-shop finds, and anything being given away, even if I didn't need it. I used to be someone who bought myself things when I was sad. But I began to feel, as many of us do at present, that all this *stuff* wasn't doing me any good. Gradually and gently, I started to shed my possessions, with the intention of keeping only the stuff I loved or had a use for, and I built a business to help other people begin to do the same. I am by no means a minimalist. My philosophy is what I like to call 'mindful

---

* Within reason. You do not have to love your colander. It does the job. Simple as.

materialism' – I love things, but I'm mindful about how they enter my life, how they are cared for, and how they leave when I no longer need them.

This process takes time, and along the way it can sometimes feel as if you're taking two steps forward and one step back, like any life adjustment. My own path to get to where I am today has not been straightforward and I have often wished for the power to put some order on the chaos. Across the last ten or so years I have been a costume designer, an events producer, a poet, a book reviewer, a psychotherapy student, a sustainable-fashion lecturer and a waitress. I've also suffered from several debilitating bouts of poor mental health which ground my life to a complete halt. I've shuttled back and forth between house shares and my family home, dragging my constantly mushrooming possessions with me. My life has been messy. But this book is not about how decluttering cured my depression. Such fairytale neatness is not possible. This book is about self-acceptance, not self-optimization. I still find unneeded things in my house that I can't seem to get rid of. I call them the 'sticky items'. And that is absolutely fine. Perfect is the enemy of better. If we can better understand our patterns of shopping and hoarding, actually use and appreciate our possessions, and be kinder to ourselves, our jam-packed lives might become a bit more manageable and a bit more peaceful, even if the world around us continues to be chaotic.

I have not only lived this process, I've studied it. At the London College of Fashion, I immersed myself in the history of clothes and their cultural importance, but also more broadly in the history of stuff and how we interact with objects. It turns out that wanting stuff is a fundamental part of our humanity and not something to be written off completely as an ill of the modern age. Humans have desired objects for both practical and fun purposes for centuries; they help mark our status and create our identity, bond us to each other through gift-giving, and hold important places in both religious and secular rituals (think wedding rings and birthday candles). There is nothing unnatural or dangerous about this desire in principle. However, my research also plunged me head first into the world of sustainable consumption and the shocking reality of the modern fashion industry. It is a useful and terrifying example of how the modern global system of mass production and cheap products is hurting people all over the world and affecting how we value what we own. Crucially, I never quite got on board with the all-possessions-are-corrupting-and-evil branch of sustainability advocacy. I learned that, while it's easy to dismiss *all* consumerism as wasteful and selfish, this is far too simplistic an argument. My approach as a decluttering consultant has grown out of this understanding of the pitfalls of capitalism but also from a respect and appreciation for the items with which we share our lives.

It's so important to understand why we shop and why we find it so hard to get rid of stuff. I have woven this information throughout the book so it can be digested easily. I have also included stories of clients I have worked with (details have been altered slightly to respect their privacy) in the hope that they may help you notice any unhelpful patterns in your own life. Some habits are universal, but it is important to note that when it comes to reorganizing your home after a declutter, I have seen again and again that no two households are the same. This is crucial to mention because too many home-organization books present broad descriptions of 'personality types', as if we all fit into neat little behavioural boxes. I would be foolish to prescribe one strict anti-clutter regime that all readers should apply to their homes, as it would likely only work for the group of people who have a personality similar to my own. I'll explain later why hyper-organized homes do not work for everyone, and it has nothing to do with laziness. The key is finding a system that works for you and those who share your space.

Why does any of this matter? Isn't having a few items of clothing that you never wear small fry in a world full of far bigger problems? I believe that it matters a great deal. At a basic level, the state of our homes can occupy way more mental real estate than is healthy. I want my clients and readers to spend their mental energy on their work, their passion projects and, most importantly, their families and communities. An overhaul of how we shop and how we value what we own can also lead to a household producing a lighter environmental footprint. This is more important than ever, given the magnitude of the environmental crisis that our planet is facing. One thing I've learned is that trying to encourage people to be more sustainable for purely environmental reasons is hard to do. That motivation usually only works if someone is already in a position of social and economic privilege. What I have spent the last decade believing is that if you can learn to understand how the wasteful and cruel capitalist system is bad for *your* wallet and *your* well-being, then you can get motivated to change. This belief was why I focused my academic research on the damaging effects of fast fashion on young consumers, and it's why I'm writing this book ten years later.

During the Covid-19 crisis, many of us became intimately acquainted with our home in a way that we never had before. It was a time of huge grief and anxiety. But it was also a time for reflection, for slowing down. Many people around me reported feeling a renewed sense of gratitude for what they already had, and that their desire for more had lessened. Many of us made more conscious choices when shopping for food and other goods, and there was a national effort to support local businesses through the crisis. This behaviour is predicted to continue into the post-virus future. I hope those predictions turn out to be correct.

Decluttering won't make you happy. What it can do is clear some space in both your home and your head. I'm not promising you spiritual enlightenment. I think the concept of pursuing permanent happiness is flawed. But if there is one thing I do preach, it is self-acceptance. It's human nature to constantly strive for better, but better happens in waves, not tsunamis. I want people to feel more content with their lives, not less. Life will always be messy, but I know one thing – you'll feel better once you've got rid of that old Tupperware that's haunting your kitchen press. I'm here to help. Join me on the long and winding journey to a life less cluttered.

Part One:
Where to Begin

I

Are You Ready?

It is often said that a good start is half the work. This is definitely true when it comes to decluttering. This first part of the book will look at preparing yourself for a successful declutter, and also how to get the process started in the most efficient and stress-free way possible.

Getting yourself ready for a declutter is not just about having enough bin bags to hand, or even setting aside enough time. It is so important that you take some time before you start to acknowledge any feelings that you fear will come up through the declutter. I can see very quickly if someone I'm working with has not prepared themselves emotionally for the decluttering process, and this can often lead to frustration. Sometimes a client looks nervous and a little embarrassed when they open their front door. They are worried that I'll judge their home or that their clutter will be the worst I've seen. Shame is a big problem for so many of us and it's an issue I'll explore in more detail later in the book.

Whatever way you feel about your home, the first step is to forgive yourself for any fault you lay at your own door. Life is hectic and even the best of us can let jobs and clutter pile up. Your clutter is *not* a reflection of you as a person. It is an aspect of your life that may benefit from improvement, but you are still more than good enough, just as you are. Take a deep breath, breathe out that guilt and relax.

It is important that you are honest with yourself about your readiness to complete this task. One client of mine was being forced to sell her home and was so full of anger and grief that she was unable to make any decisions. The session was a failure and she became furious with me for making suggestions about what to give away. The experience was understandably emotional for her, but she was unable to listen to my reassurances. She was stuck in her own anger and felt that the process was a waste of time. As I will explain later on, the human mind is a warren of hidden emotions, and understanding ourselves fully is a next-to-impossible task. But do your best to get yourself ready for what can be a long and emotional process.

Another factor which may cause pre-decluttering anxiety is the fear of change. Well-worn patterns, ways of doing things and systems for running our homes can make us feel safe, and changing them can be daunting. My advice is not to focus on what you might lose from a declutter but instead think about what you are gaining – more headspace, more organization, more freedom. Know why you're putting yourself through it, keep your thoughts on that goal and refer to it if you have a setback. Maybe even write out your goal and pin it on the wall of whatever room you're working on if you're struggling to get started.

Is everyone else ready?

There can sometimes be resistance amongst family members to decluttering. For example, if one member of a household appears to be blind to clutter, or if one sibling feels a parent's house needs to be dealt with immediately after a death and other family members are not ready. This is very sensitive territory and will require the kind of open discussion from which most people (in Ireland and the UK anyway) run a mile. Be sensitive to those around you and try to make everyone in the household as prepared as they can be for the process.

The main thing to understand about a relationship, both in terms of decluttering and in all aspects of life, is that it's impossible to change people. They can change on their own, and you can change, but you cannot *force* change upon someone else. I say this because I've had clients who have felt let down by their family's lack of enthusiasm about their decluttering project. Apathetic teenagers, worried parents and clutter-blind partners can all place extra strain on a declutter process. Accept that you can never please everyone and just paddle your own canoe. It's also important to ask ourselves if having to shoulder the burden of a cluttered space is – well – *fair.*

Don't play the blame game

Decluttering can be a stressful process, so be careful not to take it out on innocent family members. Recognize if you yourself are the source of clutter in the house and absolve your family accordingly. I learned this lesson when I suggested rehousing a set of face-paints my husband, Danny, had bought for a friend's child's party. Danny is about as non-materialistic as they come, and often even struggles to justify buying himself new clothes. But in this instance, his face fell and he gently said, 'I think I have quite a low-clutter footprint, could we not keep them?' He was right. Any clutter that arrives in our house is usually, ironically, my doing. Realizing this made future tidying conversations far easier. Developing self-awareness is a constant practice, both for decluttering and for maintaining relationships with those we love.

The mental load

A cluttered environment has the potential to fry the nerves of any household. One study of heterosexual couples directly linked cluttered homes with rising cortisol (the stress hormone) levels in women.[1] These findings were presented under the title 'For Better or Worse?' and they shine a light on the glaring gender inequality at the heart of many households. If men did the same level of housework as the women in their lives, they shared the same stress levels. More often than not, however, the study found that it was women who still bore the brunt of managing the household and thus suffered worse home-related stress. In heterosexual relationships, it appears the idea that the female partner holds the ultimate responsibility for the home is alive and well,

even in supposedly liberal and 'woke' circles. This phenomenon is widely documented and is called the 'mental load' or
the 'second shift' (a term coined by sociologist Arlie Russell
Hochschild). It basically means that the woman is the
default manager of the household. Even if her partner
'helps' her by doing things like taking out the bins, washing
up, cooking, and so on, the onus is on her to hold in her
mind all that needs to be done to allow the house and family to function smoothly. This problem can explode if a
couple have children, particularly if both of them work full
time. If a man has to ask his partner what needs to be done
in the house, or if he ignores the obvious chores that need
completing because they are not usually his job, he assumes
(sometimes unconsciously) that his partner is the one who
carries the to-do list of the house. Until both partners take
full responsibility for running the home, this mental load
remains with the woman.

Some imbalances and old-fashioned gender roles are
more explicit. There is a horrible episode of *Tidying Up with
Marie Kondo* where Rachel (a stay-at-home mother) and her
husband, Kevin (a sales manager), seek Kondo's help to
declutter their home as a way to help ease the tension in
their relationship and resolve their housekeeping-related
fights. Kevin chides Rachel for paying a housekeeper to do
laundry when he believes that 'we're perfectly capable of
doing those things'. Rachel explains the challenges of feeding and clothing the children and that all she wants is a tiny
bit of help with the laundry. Kevin seems to find this
unacceptable; reality was not living up to his dream of being
with a 1950s housewife.

This might sound like I think all men are selfish and lazy, which is absolutely not the case. I happen to be married to a man who does as much (if not more) housework as me, without ever being asked to. Sadly, however, it has been proven that an unequal distribution of domestic work between men and women is the default for many households. The huge success of the 2018 book *The Mental Load* by French comic-book writer Emma (it's not me pretending to be French, I promise) is testament to this. There are some who even suggest that the trend for decluttering and obsessively cleaning your house fetishizes these seemingly intractable gender roles. I think feminism is about choice, and if a fair and respectful decision is made within a couple about one person taking more responsibility for household work, it's really none of my business. But if an imbalance is becoming a strain on your relationship, do your best to address it. This is far easier said than done, particularly when childcare is involved.

Older relatives

Many people are eager to help older relatives clear out their houses. It is common for adult children to find themselves in the position of witnessing an older relative lose control over their space but be reluctant to change. Although the intention may be good, encouraging an older relative or friend to clear out their home can be tricky. Try to be conscious of the ways in which the process may be stressful for them. If there is a resistance on their part, I suggest reframing the aim of the task. The word 'declutter' might imply that some of their possessions are rubbish, a view to which they may object. Suggesting that you work together to make the house or apartment safer or more comfortable can work. If possible, try not to rush people into making decisions. Explaining that the process may be emotional might also be met with resistance; older generations can sometimes view millennials' obsession with 'feelings' and emotions as jarring and frivolous. Start with small projects framed as positively as possible and take it from there.

Over-decluttering

Over-decluttering is definitely something to watch out for. I have seen several backlash articles against Marie Kondo, bestselling author of *The Life-Changing Magic of Tidying Up* and arguably the best-known decluttering professional, where the panicked writers are regretting their purges, having been left with no clothes to wear because none 'sparked joy'. It's tricky territory, this, because I very much want to discourage holding on to things unnecessarily, but I also want to advise you to approach decluttering with a level head.

Aoife's story

I had a client a few years ago who was embarking on a career change. She had been a costume designer like myself and was now retraining as a primary-school teacher. She was moving house and urgently needed to go through the papers she had accumulated over a fifteen-year career in the arts. I could see as we started that she was anxious about the process but was determined to see it through. There were several points at which she became emotional and I asked if she would rather stop, but she kept going. At the end of the session there were three large bags of programmes, cards and letters which were to be recycled the next day. That evening she sent me a message to say that she had been too hasty and needed it all back. I was saddened to hear her distress, but unsurprised. I was also annoyed with myself for not reining in her ruthlessness, but it can be difficult to stop someone who seems determined and in control. I've also learned from experience never to throw things away until forty-eight hours have passed since I've been with a client. If you are worried that you'll regret your decluttering decisions, keep the charity-shop bags somewhere out of sight, for example in the car, if you have one, or in a hall cupboard. Resist at all costs the attempt to go back through the bags, but if any particular item does occur to you as vitally important over the next day or two, you have the opportunity to retrieve it.

Yo-yo decluttering

I will admit that I have been caught in a cycle of yo-yo decluttering in the past, and I can see that many of my clients have been too. They have decluttering and home-organization books on their shelves but have fallen off the wagon again and again. This is not because they are weak-willed or naturally messy. It is because the root causes of the problem – how we accumulate too much in the first place – have not been addressed. Marie Kondo's idea that you can clean up once and never have to do it again is dishonest. Decluttering a life is like unpacking Russian matryoshka dolls; you have to go through several layers before you are done. I do not say this to make the process any more daunting than it already seems. I say it because it is the reality. By peeling back the layers slowly, and at the same time addressing your shopping habits (which we'll get into later on), what you really want to have in your life and what you really use will emerge.

Conclusion

So far, we have covered some of the initial pitfalls that can hamper the decluttering process, such as relationship tensions and emotional readiness. Diving into a declutter without considering these factors can lead to rows, stress and unwise decisions. I mention emotional labour because I believe so many women's burdens are still hushed up, out of sight. If this section brought up emotion for you, take your time to process those feelings as best you can. As I'll repeat throughout the book, there's way more to decluttering than just getting rid of stuff. For now, let's move on to the practical dos and don'ts of starting a declutter off on the right foot.

2

Getting Started

A cluttered room is like a blank page for a writer – daunting. Where to begin? What I have learned over the past few years of decluttering work is that no household or family is the same. All of my clients have unique quirks and ways of doing things, from strange names for the remote control and the utility room, to elaborate laundry systems which are unintelligible to me but work for them. This chapter explains how to structure an efficient declutter session. It can and should be chopped, changed and altered into whatever shape makes the most sense for you. There is evidence that finishing a task thanks to hints rather than specific instructions feels more rewarding, and I'm in favour of this approach. Self-help books which operate under the assumption that 'this worked for me so it will 100 per cent work for you' can promise too much and often don't acknowledge the complexity of habit and lifestyle change. But I have been around the block more than a few times with this, and here's what I've learned.

Finding the time

Our lives are cluttered with commitments. Often, it can feel like our time is not our own. Taking back this control is one aspect of the mental decluttering I suggest at the end of the book but, for now, I offer my advice on tackling the problem of finding the time to declutter. A client who was struggling with her health hired me for one half-day every week for a number of weeks. This worked well and we achieved what she wanted. But my instinct is always to try, as best you can, to set aside full days for this work. You build momentum that is lost if you are only snatching hours here and there. Put it in the diary and stick to it. There's never a *right time* to do this. As with any project, if you wait for the perfect conditions, it may never happen.

Day one checklist

Now, if there's one thing I want you to take away from this chapter, it is this decree: DO NOT BUY STORAGE BEFORE YOU DECLUTTER. Storage bought before shedding unwanted stuff can become clutter in its own right. Empty boxes and bags contain some sort of black magic which attracts items, regardless of their value. Once clutter has found a home in your well-intentioned storage boxes, it becomes part of the backdrop to life and is very difficult to budge. I see it so often in clients, who think, 'Well, there's room for it, so why not keep it?', even if the item is disliked or never used. I repeat: do not buy storage! The only things you need to start shedding your unwanted stuff are:

- Black bags for the following destinations:
  - Charity shop
  - Paper that requires shredding
  - Non-paper recycling, e.g. electronics
  - Landfill
- A recycling bag for paper, cardboard and hard plastic waste
- A few tote bags or a cardboard box for items that need to be moved to other rooms
- A cardboard box for sentimental items like cards, children's art and letters
- Sticky labels and a thick marker pen
- A damp cloth for cleaning as you go – you'd be amazed at the dust you find when decluttering. Did you know that the collective noun for spiders is 'a clutter'? Be warned.
- Comfortable clothes
- A can-do attitude

Start small

It is natural to feel overwhelmed by a large project. Let me share with you a phrase which I use in my daily life that I find calming and helpful: 'bird by bird'. This little phrase is the title of a highly respected creative-writing guide by novelist Anne Lamott: *Bird by Bird: Some Instructions on Writing and Life*. It comes from a story which Lamott remembers from her childhood:

> Thirty years ago my older brother, who was ten years old at the time, was trying to get a report on birds written that he'd had three months to write. It was due the next day. We were out at our family cabin in Bolinas, and he was at the kitchen table close to tears, surrounded by binder paper and pencils and unopened books on birds, immobilized by the hugeness of the task ahead. Then my father sat down beside him, put his arm around my brother's shoulder, and said, 'Bird by bird, buddy. Just take it bird by bird.'[2]

One of my many mantras, this phrase never fails to get me into a calm and productive state of mind.

Everyone approaches a daunting decluttering project differently. Some might prefer to tackle a small and easy task first thing in the morning; others might want to plunge into the worst item on their list to get it over with. In my opinion, a good place to start is the hotpress/airing cupboard, or wherever your towels and sheets are, or else a bedside table. It is up to you, and I would encourage you to go with your instincts on this (but be careful to maintain your energy, as I'll explain below).

In my experience, a small task like clearing a bedside cabinet or one particular drawer is the perfect way to ease you into the choppy waters of a day of decluttering. You will get a great sense of achievement early on, which will keep you going, and you are less likely to encounter potentially distracting sentimental items amongst old towels. Another good task to start with is to clear any obvious rubbish, like waste paper or food, from a space. With one layer down and your momentum up and running, you can then move on to more complex decisions.

Some experts offer a precise order in which to tackle each item, but I find that different households have different problems and goals. For example, I had a client whose main problem was her filing system, which was completely overloaded and causing her huge anxiety. Once this was tackled, weeded and properly organized, she could see far more clearly what she wanted to keep in other areas of the house. The only rule I have in terms of order is to always leave sentimental items until last. If you come across old letters, photos or cards, place them in the designated cardboard box and put them to one side. This is because paying too much attention to these items can bring up emotions which may derail the process. Even if you don't realize it at the time, seeing an old photograph can stir things up in your subconscious, and it is important to create the appropriate space to process these feelings when going through personal memorabilia. Items will inevitably come up which you'll have to deal with on the spot, such as in your wardrobe, but try to stick to the general rule of leaving sentimental items for a time when you can calmly process them. This would ideally be separate from the more humdrum task of sorting everyday items.

Clutter hotspots

Clutter is like a weed: it can breed uncontrollably if left unchecked for too long. Try and take a minute before you start to pinpoint the clutter hotspots in your home. Examples include innocent-looking junk drawers, kitchen counters, coffee tables, and so on. Each house will have its own flow of clutter. It's one thing to declutter these areas once, and it's quite another to stop stuff building up again over time. Finding the *flow* of your home sounds a bit *woo woo*, but it can really help to stop the clutter piles from creeping back in. Ask yourself:

- Where do I dump things when I come in the door, and does that habit work?
- Where do I leave things that I don't want to decide upon immediately?
- How can I shift my clutter hotspots?

Clutter is not a category, it is a delayed decision. There is a bowl in my house, just inside the front door, which holds my keys, wallet, headphones, letters to be dealt with, anything I take out of my bag at the end of the day. It currently also contains a scrap of fabric from my wedding dress, a lighter and a pot of lip balm. These bowls or boxes or drawers are okay, as long as you only have one of them in each room. My rule is that if it starts to overflow, I have to go through it and redistribute items to their proper homes. If an item seems wedded to a particular clutter-spot because you can't think of anywhere else to put it, take some time to think properly about where it should be stored. Try not to leave clutter somewhere simply out of indecision or lack of imagination about where it could live. The solution will unfold as the process goes on; you will either find a home for it, or it will become clear that it no longer has a place in your house.

Energy management

One of my main roles with a client is paying close attention to when their energy or patience is waning and to suggest a break. It is very tempting to keep going to the point of exhaustion because we just want the flaming job over with. Trust me, you will get far more done if you take scheduled breaks. I would suggest every ninety minutes, but it's up to you. It is important at this time to leave the room you're working on, not just sit there staring at the mess and gripping your coffee cup tighter and tighter with anxiety. Step outside if you can, have a drink, have a snack, listen to the radio and come back after about fifteen minutes. My task during these breaks is also to tidy up anything that doesn't require decision-making: I remove rubbish bags, wipe down surfaces, and group items into categories to make selection easier, for example, all make-up together, all stationery together, and so on. If you have someone with you to help declutter, which I would recommend, explain to them that this is their role. Your task is decision-making. Be careful in choosing your decluttering assistant. Choose someone who is practical and who isn't likely to insist that you keep things unnecessarily.

Decision fatigue is a genuine thing. Making choices is tiring and our attention wanes after a certain amount of time, causing us to make unwise decisions. You may end up keeping things that really ought to go, or throwing everything out in an exhausted fury. If this happens, you've hit the clutter wall. Imagine it: you're sitting in the middle of a room, can't see the floor for stuff, no idea how to get started again. I've been there. It happens. Take a breath. Step outside the room. You'll get back on the horse and you *will* finish the job.

Decision-making

I once gave a talk at the National Library in Dublin, which went very well until the questions at the end. After listening to my thoughts on consumerism and my advice on the emotional weight of objects, one grumpy-looking man in the second row (there's always one) raised his hand. 'But how do you *actually* get rid of stuff?' he asked, exasperated. I was mortified to have failed to communicate this, and for just a moment felt like some sort of charlatan. I managed to say: 'You have to ask yourself, will this item serve my life in the future? Do I need it, will I use it, do I like it?'

The thing is, we have a culture that is structured around accumulating stuff. We do not have, however, any social practices in place for getting rid of things. So it seems unnatural and unfamiliar to us. And that's why it's hard.

There are two categories into which items fall in my house:

- It is useful, it works and I use it; and
- I love it, it represents a part of my life and it makes me happy.

There are of course the sticky items, which require deeper questions to be asked. I'll cover these problem objects in Chapter 4.

To get started, it's best to focus on the items that simply require a yes/no answer to determine whether or not they stay. This is the first layer of clutter, if you like. The problem areas can be addressed more slowly and calmly at a later stage.

Some decluttering experts encourage their clients to touch every item in their homes to assess its value and help them make a decision, but other strategies exist with research behind them. One decluttering psychologist, Dr Joseph Ferrari, found in the course of his research that clutter is also often the result of an over-attachment to our personal items which makes it difficult to part with them. His advice is: 'if you're going to declutter, don't touch the item. Once you touch the item, you are less likely to get rid of it.'[3] My two cents on this debate is that I don't believe that you need to deliberately touch something in order to make a decision, but that some items will require handling, such as clothes or more sentimental items. I am aware, of course, that the luxury of having someone to help you declutter and to handle things for you is not open to everybody. Don't worry about this: as long as you schedule breaks and stay kind to yourself, you will be fine decluttering alone.

Conclusion

I hope you now feel equipped with enough information to give your decluttering adventure the best possible chance of success. In the next chapter, I move away from the details of a personal clear-out and discuss what made me want to write this book in the first place – the hidden causes of clutter that no one seems to want to mention: shopping, consumer culture, and the myth that money and stuff can bring us happiness. I'm going deep, because it is only by confronting these issues head-on that we have any hope of gaining some sort of control over our homes and our lives. In a world where Covid-19 exists, that confrontation is more important than ever. Like I said in the introduction, you might feel that you want to skip this stuff, but I promise you that if you trust me and read on, you will stay clutter-free for far longer!

3

Why Do We Have
So Much Stuff?

If the decluttering craze of recent years is anything to go
by, it's clear that many people who live in wealthy countries
simply have too much stuff. A key part of staying clutter-
free long-term is understanding why we have so much stuff
in the first place. This chapter takes a deep dive into the
roots of the consumer culture that fuels our cluttered lives.
We'll take a look at modern advertising and the heightened
emotional links that businesses draw between customers
and products, as well as the psychological impact this has
had on those of us who live in capitalist countries. I'll talk
about how the most primal parts of our brains are manipulated into wanting more and more by clever marketers, and
how it has been proven time and again that acquiring more
does not bring us happiness. First, we need to have a look
at the bigger picture and one of the strongest forces influ-
encing our buying behaviours: neoliberalism.

The Ladybird guide to neoliberalism

Many wealthy countries now operate within the economics of neoliberalism, a system which encourages spending and prioritizes economic growth above all else. It achieves this by persuading people to identify as consumers rather than citizens. We live to serve the market, and that means working hard and spending hard. Neoliberal ideology wants citizens to see themselves not as one part of a community but as individuals in an economic survival-of-the-fittest race for resources, status and wealth. My generation, in particular, seems to feel compelled to 'self-optimize', always striving to achieve more and be the best possible version of ourselves. It's making millions of us seriously ill and has widened the gap between the most vulnerable and poor members of society and the most powerful and wealthy.

I think neoliberalism is bad news. Thankfully, the tide is turning. The 2008 financial crisis and the previously unthinkable government interventions that halted it have discredited two central neoliberal orthodoxies: that capitalism cannot fail, and that governments cannot step in to change how the economy works. An alternative must be found. Leftist policies regarding health care and social welfare support which were rolled out by many governments during the Covid-19 crisis were a step in the right direction. But it's very early days, and who knows what ideas will stick and to what extent vested interests will push back against change. Watch this space.

We cannot stem the tide of clutter without understanding the forces that manipulate us into buying in the first place. Under neoliberalism, there are many clever tricks employed to persuade us to part with our money and accumulate things. To get us started, let's look at one of the biggest changes that has occurred in advertising over the past century: the linking of objects to emotions.

Edward Bernays – the genius who made you buy that perfume

The advertising genius Edward Bernays was a key figure in the development of modern consumer culture. Advertising in the form of fashion plates and aspirational lifestyle ads in magazines already existed before he came along, but Bernays kicked everything into a new gear. Beginning his work in the 1920s, he pioneered the field of public relations (previously referred to by the more sinister title 'propaganda'), using the tools of crowd psychology and the newly fashionable theories of psychoanalysis, which had been developed by his uncle, Sigmund Freud. Bernays believed that by tapping into the public's unconscious, desires could be implanted there, to the benefit of companies wishing to increase sales. His most ingenious innovation was to link emotions to products in order to persuade the purchaser to believe that they were buying into a newer, shinier version of themselves instead of just the product itself. If you've ever been mystified by the ridiculousness of modern perfume ads which depict mysterious and alien-like young women enjoying fantastical love affairs in flowing silk, blame Bernays. Those ads are selling a lifestyle, not a fragrance. The perfume could smell like a cheap pharmacy equivalent, but by purchasing the brand and the pretty bottle, the consumer takes what they subconsciously see as a step towards the fantasy life depicted in the cinematic ads. That's Bernays' legacy.

Bernays' most famous feat of PR has become known as the Lucky Strike cigarettes 'Torches of Freedom' campaign. He had already achieved some success in the tobacco industry by linking smoking to thinness, which helped solidify the thin ideal as the image of the perfect woman. Lucky Strike cigarettes needed him to solve another problem for them: although women smoked in their own homes, it was still seen as uncouth for a woman to be seen smoking in public, which of course was affecting sales. Bernays arranged for a number of recognizable women (but, crucially, not models, so the stunt would appear natural and unstaged) to attend the 1929 Easter Sunday parade down Fifth Avenue in New York whilst smoking Lucky Strikes. Many of the women he chose were prominent members of the women's movement, including Ruth Hale, who is said to have declared, 'Women! Light another torch of freedom! Fight another sex taboo!' The effect of this stunt was extraordinary; smoking became an act of defiance against the patriarchy, and female smokers emerged in their tens of thousands. These women of Fifth Avenue were the precursors to our current flood of online 'influencers', who also advertise products whilst sometimes forgetting to mention the fact that they are getting paid (#controversial).

Bernays' ideas became central to the entire system of commerce, radically transforming how many of us buy. In 2019 I attended a performance of the *The Lehman Trilogy*, a play that explores the history of the Lehman Brothers' bank, which collapsed in 2008, triggering the global financial crisis. In one scene, an unnamed marketing expert advises the board that the only way to save the bank after the 1929 Wall Street Crash is to convince people to *buy*; to teach citizens that buying is an *instinct* instead of simply a means to fulfil a need. This would encourage people to seek out more money and, subsequently, because the banks offered greater and greater lines of credit with which to buy now and pay later, the economy was stabilized in the short term and the marketplace, which lost nearly $400 billion in today's money, began trading again. Think of how radical a shift that was. The transformation of shopping from a neutral everyday task to an activity that was suddenly an integral part of being human. I suspect that the unnamed character onstage was Bernays himself.

The myth of 'consumer demand'

What Bernays achieved was built on in the following decades with the explosion of the advertising and marketing industries. Another key idea which developed was that human needs were not set in stone, they could be created through clever marketing. In the anti-capitalist Dr Seuss book *The Lorax*, this trick is explained though the storyline of the must-have object: the Thneed. A Thneed is a highly versatile knitted object which is described by its inventor as 'a-fine-something-that-all-people-need'. It is not something anyone wanted or needed, but the idea that everyone needs a Thneed (get it?) catches on like wildfire. I would highly recommend the 2012 animated film of the book, particularly for teaching children about this stuff.

In real life, my favourite (or should I say most hated) example of a 'need' which was created to sell us stuff was the 'need' to get rid of cellulite. Cellulite was invented by journalist Nicole Ronsard in 1973. I say 'invented', but of course it already existed because – and I cannot emphasize this enough – it is simply the behaviour of normal adult skin. What was invented was the idea that it was a problem that needed fixing. *Allegedly* fixable problems can sell stuff fast, so Ronsard became a millionaire and millions of women still hate a part of their body for no reason other than someone's wish to encourage them to buy products. I'll talk more about body image and capitalism in Chapters 7 and 8; it is an area I never cease to be enraged by.

New needs are invented all the time, with corporations defending themselves by claiming that they are simply responding to our desires, as if their hands were tied and they only ever had our best interests at heart, rather than their bottom line. Consumer demand is often touted as the reason companies began producing more and more products for cheaper and cheaper prices (with lower and lower quality and involving worse and worse humanitarian and environmental practices). This is untrue. It is a lie put forth by corporations who want to seem blameless for the waste and damage they create. Johan Stenebo, who held

senior positions in Ikea for over twenty years, put it suc-
cinctly in a 2020 interview with the *Guardian*:

> Get the prices down and you increase sales – we created
> the demand, not the consumer. He also highlights how
> blame for the environmental impact of the mass produc-
> tion of stuff is often wrongly shifted to the consumer; he
> says that climate change is corporate-driven but we always
> talk about consumer behaviour.[4]

We, the consumers, did not demand, want or need the
disposable society created for us by corporate greed. And
yet, so often, an unwillingness to change supply-chain
practices and means of production is claimed to be down
to keeping consumers happy. It's not, and we have the
power to let companies know that by adopting better shopping habits and becoming more informed and engaged
consumers and citizens.

Money can't buy happiness

The emotional link which Bernays drew between possessions and personal fulfilment has proven false, as he
always knew it to be. Accumulating possessions does not
bring lasting happiness, and the highs of material wealth
are short-lived beyond a certain point of financial comfort. The figure at which happiness in relation to annual
income plateaus is approximately $75,000 (roughly £60,000,

or €69,000), according to a 2010 study from researchers at Princeton University.[5] The actual number is not significant; what's important is the finding that increasing wealth stops increasing our happiness after a certain point. The study revealed that the lower a person's annual income falls below that benchmark, the unhappier they may feel. But no matter how much more than $75,000 people make, they don't report any greater degree of well-being. They may feel a superficial increase in status, but their day-to-day happiness remains stable. The appeal and power of Bernays' theory remains, however, because it offers a fantasy whereby the stresses of life can be dulled by believing that purchasing the next gadget, holiday, kitchen, or whatever, will lead us closer to lasting happiness.

This is one of the most warped ideas that consumerism sells us – the belief that we will someday increase our happiness levels by gaining material wealth and rising up the ranks ahead of our peers. Another scientific finding has emerged which proves that our happiness is even *further* removed from material wealth than the Princeton study shows.[6] Here's the truth bomb that I found difficult to process when I first heard it:

Your happiness level is set and relatively immovable.

Let that sink in. Now let me explain.

In 2005, researchers at the Norwegian Institute of Public Health found that happiness depends on three key ingredients:

- Genetic inheritance
- Life circumstances
- Intentional activity

Genetics counts for 50 per cent, but life circumstances constitute only 10 per cent of what makes up our level of happiness. Factors like an adequate income, a stable relationship, good family dynamics, a good job, health, being religious, and so on, have relatively little effect on overall happiness. So even that benchmark of $75,000 may be irrelevant if your genetic make-up is skewed sharply one way or the other.

The remaining 40 per cent are things we choose to do and actually do, such as:

- What we pay attention to in our lives
- Our mindset or attitude
- How we choose to spend our time outside work
- The goals we set and pursue

Infuriatingly, even though our base level of happiness is set like a thermostat, we are all driven to endlessly strive for more than we currently have. This can lead us to getting trapped on what is called the 'hedonic treadmill', or happiness treadmill. This is basically the following cycle:

Desire – gratification – boredom – desire

We decide we want something, we get it and feel satisfied, we get used to it and get bored, we desire more again. Multiple studies have shown that we are often happiest at the anticipation stage of acquiring something. We think we want a new coat, we look at what's available, we dream of how we'll feel whilst wearing the new coat and we excitedly buy the coat. But after a short period of time the coat fades into the background of our lives and the itch for something *new* returns. Humans are wired to adapt to change swiftly. This is the same process which leads lottery winners to return to their original level of life satisfaction, presumably after a period of mad spending. I observed this cycle in nearly all of the interviewees for my fast-fashion research, all of whom were young women in their twenties and thirties. Several of them told me that they were actually happier when shopping than when wearing the clothes out in the world. It's not only these brief thrills that keep us hooked on shopping; we've also been taught that what we own can help us tell the world exactly who we are.

I shop therefore I am

Creating a solid sense of identity is important for all humans, but it's not always a simple task. In the past, it may have been easier to establish your identity as part of a religious group, a profession, a community or a particular economic class – all of which seemed relatively stable. These days, we almost have whiplash with the speed of change around issues like life-long employment, long-term marriage and organized religion. These social shifts are not necessarily negative, but one consequence (with some help from neo-liberalism) is that, gradually, many people learned to view themselves as individuals, rather than as connected members of a community. We began to assess ourselves based on our own personal value and not by the value we contribute to the group as a whole. This has left people feeling very unsure about how to construct their identities. Enter Bernays' marketing tactics, which are particularly powerful and influential on members of a society which is in a constant state of change.

A solution to this anxiety regarding our place within the community was provided by consumer capitalism. What's a quick-fix way to show your status? Buy a car that's bigger than your neighbours' car, or the must-have handbag of the season. Economist Tim Jackson put it perfectly when he said, 'In rich countries today, consumption consists of people spending money they don't have to buy things they don't want to impress people they don't care about.' Over time, we have been taught to think of ourselves as unique individuals, and that we can express our individualism and success through what we own. We have been simultaneously drawn to asserting our place within a group by obtaining the *correct* items, which were also desired and owned by our peers. This tension between wanting to be unique but also wanting to conform is the plight of every teenager, but it extends well into adulthood.

A primal drive which we all share is the desire to be part of the group. There is a small percentage of humans who are genetically adventurous and independent, something that would have benefited early societies as a whole when these people returned to the fold, having discovered a fresh-water supply, or pineapples, or whatever. Mostly, humans want to be snug within a group they recognize and they want to assert their status within that group. When capitalists and marketers made shopping the hot new activity, not to shop was to be outside the group. 'Conspicuous consumption', a term coined in the 1890s, is the psychology behind the insatiable appetite for designer logos printed on everything from lunchboxes to snowboards. It's a gorilla-like chest-thump to say, 'Me big and strong, me have Smeg fridge and Balenciaga handbag.'

Even for the vast majority who cannot afford designer brands, to be seen having the *right* stuff gives us a sense of calm. Increasingly, the best way to be seen to conspicuously consume is to have constant *new* things as well as the *correct* things. For younger generations, this is particularly the case in their attitudes to clothing. Many young people do not want to be seen in the same outfit twice. This is conspicuous consumption on speed. I learned this first hand when I ran ethical-fashion workshops for highly disinterested teenage students. I would enthusiastically explain sweatshops and the drawbacks of constantly buying cheap, disposable garments, and they would stare back with derision in their eyes, probably thinking about whether or not their Pretty Little Thing order would arrive in time for the weekend. It has been some time since I have worked with schools, and I would hope that the rise of Greta Thunberg and the global school climate strike movement may have increased young people's interest in sustainability. But social change happens slowly, and I fear it may be some time before teenagers give up their devotion to ethically dubious online fashion retailers.

Despite study after study proving that our happiness levels have not been affected by increased economic success, we are repeatedly reminded that living in this economy means spending, accumulating and achieving, displaying our wealth as a marker of our status and identity. Shopping, we are told, can give us a sense of control in an increasingly hostile and chaotic world. It doesn't, but it does tap into some primal drives over which we have no control. And that is why it's so hard to stop.

The messiness of the human mind

Most of us like to think that we are not fooled by marketing and advertising tactics – after all, we're pretty savvy about the media nowadays, not lemmings mindlessly following every new idea, aren't we? The truth is that our primal drives should not be underestimated; we're still mammals who used to be reptiles and our brains are still scanning the horizon for dangers and seeking out the best ways to survive and thrive. Clever marketeers know this and have learned exactly how to tap into these drives in order to urge us to keep buying.

The closer I look at my own thoughts and behaviour, the more I believe that being human is like driving a car with no hands. We have so little access to what is actually going on in our minds at any one moment. The human mind is a mess of tangled memories, primal drives and mysterious and mercurial reactions.

Marketing teams and PR gurus are smart folks. They

know how to bury their ideas in the deepest parts of our subconscious minds and to sow seeds where we won't even notice them growing. Sometimes this can be so subtle that we might believe we've had the idea to buy something or eat something all by ourselves. You know the weird feeling you get when you buy a new piece of clothing which you feel reflects your own personal style and then, soon, you see it everywhere? I know I'm not alone in this. That's the power of subliminal marketing at play. Modern marketers are the descendants of the Edward Bernays school of psychology: tap into people's deepest fears and desires and keep them hooked on the dopamine high (dopamine is the brain's pleasure hormone) they get from spending and buying.

The evolutionary roots of consumption

When I very briefly studied psychology, I was shocked by how little is actually understood about the way the brain operates. Let's explore what we *do* know about the parts of the human brain that are involved in desire and decision-making, that is, the parts which are targeted by advertising. I have simplified things, but the explanation below will do for our purposes and I think it's really important to know this stuff so we can understand why it can be so tough to stop bringing clutter into our homes.

The brain stem is the oldest part of the brain and it manages the body's most basic functions, like our breathing and our heart rate. Next comes our limbic system, which is where the magic happens. The limbic system is essentially our invisible puppet-master, the driver of our emotional reactions and memories. If you've ever cried over a seemingly harmless advert because it reminded of you something in your childhood, the limbic system was responsible. It trips us up all the time, in arguments which make us revert to childhood patterns of conflict, in strange fears we can't get to the bottom of, in overly emotional reactions we can't explain.

The prefrontal cortex is the part of our brain that has evolved most recently and is tasked with keeping the other two primitive and impulsive parts in check. Like a team which has worked together successfully for millennia suddenly being overseen by a new boss, the stubborn brain stem and limbic systems often override the supposedly 'rational' prefrontal cortex. The scary part is that we have no idea this rebellion is happening. We aim to act and react rationally and calmly, but our brains often have other ideas. And one of the key responsibilities of this new and inexperienced system is to exert willpower and self-control.

Willpower is one of the newer accessories to arrive with the prefrontal cortex. It often fails dramatically to silence our impulses for food, violence, sex and, most recently, buying stuff, because it's just not up to the task yet. Here's what I really want to stress: capitalism and consumer culture are very recent phenomena in the history of our species. Desire and the drive to accumulate things, to assert our status in the group and to seek pleasure are as old as the limbic system. We are wired to strive for more and more. It's what kept our ancestors alive, kept them copulating and helped them build, for better or worse, the world we live in today. So your desire for more stuff, more money, a bigger house, and so on, isn't individual covetousness, it's pretty natural! It's just the toxic cocktail of basic survival drives and consumer capitalism that has us in the polluted and cluttered mess in which we find ourselves.

Conclusion

All the above may seem like a messy state of affairs, and in many ways it is. But the cure for the ill lies at the root of the problem. If we can understand the strange forces at play in the world around us, we can develop more resistance and not be so in thrall to the promises of consumer capitalism. Now, when I find myself wanting to buy something, I have the knowledge and sense to stop and ask questions before I take the plunge. I continue to be fascinated by the messiness of the mind and do my best to relax into its unpredictability. In my experience with both decluttering and mental health maintenance, self-awareness is key. In the next chapter, we'll explore the emotional blocks that can arise when you are decluttering particularly difficult items. If we can learn to identify them, they will become easier to unpick.

Part Two:
Getting Stuck In

4

How to Tackle Sticky Items

Some decluttering choices are clear cut and others require mental gymnastics to reach a decision. This chapter deals with what I call the 'sticky items', which require a more complex level of inquiry than just asking ourselves, 'Do I like this?' and 'Do I use it?' Once upon a time, I was the queen of dreaming up justifications for keeping things. My scraps of paper and fabric were 'useful', the dress that never fitted quite right had been 'expensive', the ugly jumper was 'a gift' and the giant bag of teddies was 'sentimental'. I really have been there. What I've also found is that the longer something has been in the house, the more you feel inclined to keep it. We need to explore what is blocking us from making concrete decisions about these sticky items and understand the emotions at play under the surface of our indecision.

Expensive items

Expense is an excuse I hear time and time again from clients, friends and family, so let's use an example to break it down. You have a juice-maker in the shed. It is an old model, difficult to clean and possibly broken. You no longer make juice and have no plans to return to your liquid lunches. Every time you go to clear out the shed, the juicer remains because 'it was expensive' and is 'high quality'. This is what is known as a sunk cost. The money is spent, you will never get it back, and having the offending item sitting there staring at you will not change that. This excuse is about shame. We feel we have done something wrong by spending our precious income on an item we don't use. We cannot face admitting this mistake and so never make a definite decision.

I tripped up in this way many times, for example with a coat I owned for years that had cost me more than I would like to say. It was well cut, in nice fabric and from a good label. Although it never looked right on me, I could not get rid of it. I even wore it to a wedding once, simply to justify my keeping it. In the photos I look uncomfortable, as if I'm trying to hide in the stupid coat. I recently, finally, passed it on to a friend who I know will love it. I had a similar experience with a pair of black Converse runners which I'd kept from my waitressing days. I no longer wanted to wear them, but they were *good* leather and my justification for their place in my wardrobe was that I would someday need them for hillwalking (who goes hiking in Converse?) or some sort of fantasy DIY project. I finally brought them to a clothes swap a few months ago, and feel the lighter for it. Sometimes it takes time for the grip of certain possessions to loosen. Like an annoying house guest who outstays their welcome, one day you will come to your senses and ask them to leave.

Try using this process to get rid of expensive items you no longer need:

1. Be brutally honest and ask yourself if you are ever going to use it again or if you are going to change your lifestyle so that it becomes useful.
2. If the answer is no, then please forgive yourself for spending the money. It's okay: it happens to the best of us.
3. Pass the unused item on responsibly.
4. Use this as an opportunity to commit to making wiser purchases in the future.

Reselling

Many clients ask about reselling expensive items. This can be a useful and sustainable way of rehoming devices and furniture, but be warned, you will not get the resale price you expect for your things. If reselling is motivated by wanting to recoup lost costs, it may make you feel worse when you realize how little cash you end up with after postage. The best way to make up for money lost is to accept it, forgive yourself and let the guilt go. I recently came across an article slating the 1990s Beanie Babies investment craze (which I lived through but did not participate in) as a sham. If cash is tight, by all means try and get a couple of quid back by selling, but remember to be kind to yourself throughout this process and avoid beating yourself up about past spending mistakes.

Useful items

The perception of something being generally 'useful', even if it is languishing unused, is another big justification for clutter that many of us fall victim to. 'It'll come in handy someday' is a refrain I hear all too often in the course of my work. I find myself asking, 'Handy for whom?' While we are all more aware than ever of how important it is to avoid creating unnecessary waste and keep stuff out of landfill, having items sitting in our homes unused is also wasteful. These resources should be given to others to help them avoid unnecessary future purchases. Having the materials we need for day-to-day living easily within reach is a normal desire, but many people take it to an extreme level. Hoarding old orphaned wires, battered garden tools, never-used kitchenware, and so on, 'because they are useful' can stem from a sense of scarcity and fear experienced by previous generations. During the course of my research I came across *three* articles written by men bemoaning the fact that their Kondo-crazed partners were forcing them to give up their useless old wires. This appears to be a particular fixation for men of a certain age, and I can only attribute it to fear of scarcity. It is a phenomenon that requires further investigation.

Why decluttering can bring up fear

Humans fear losing things far more than they desire gaining them. Fearing loss harks back to one of our earliest survival goals, which was to never be without essential resources like food, shelter, social bonds, and so on. Basic brain-stem stuff. For us modern-day humans, this fear extends beyond our basic survival into many other aspects of our lives. The phenomenon was demonstrated in a Nobel Prize-winning piece of work from behavioural psychologists Daniel Kahneman and Amos Tversky in the 1990s. They called their theory 'aversion to loss'.

According to Kahneman and Tversky, losses have a greater emotional impact than a gain of the equivalent amount. In simple terms, we dislike losing more than we like winning. Where decluttering is concerned, the most fascinating offshoot of aversion to loss is something called the 'endowment effect', whereby we think an object that we already own has more value than a similar item that we do not. One of the most famous experiments into the endowment effect was carried out in 1990 by Daniel Kahneman, Jack Knetsch and Richard Thaler.[7] In this study, some of the participants were given a mug. They were not told the retail price of the mug and were asked to list the lowest price they'd be willing to sell it for. Other participants didn't receive a mug but instead were asked how much they'd be willing to pay to buy the mug given to the first participants. The difference in price from each group for the same mug was striking: those with the mug listed selling prices that were too high for the buyers (on average, they would not sell for less than $5.25). In contrast, those buying the mug did not want to pay more than $2.25–$2.75. This experiment was repeated with other objects, including pens. Even when the price tag was left on the pen, the same effect was demonstrated, with pen sellers listing sale prices of \$4.25–\$4.75, even when the pen's price tag showed \$3.98.

The endowment effect explains why it can be very hard for us to get rid of things that we already own. By becoming aware of this phenomenon, I hope we might find it easier to disentangle ourselves from items we don't need or want but keep because of this proven psychological quirk which we all experience. A useful question to ask yourself if you are struggling with an item is: 'Would I buy this if I saw it in a shop today?' This can help you understand if you truly like or need the item, or if it is being kept because of your fear of losing it.

Aversion to loss affects not just our decluttering decisions but our shopping choices too.

Adverts for sales and discounts literally go through our eyes into the oldest part of our brain and scream, 'Scarcity!' Resource scarcity would have been a very serious matter for our ancestors, and our limbic system is oblivious to the triviality of discounted eye-shadow. All it registers is that scarcity equals danger and danger must be avoided. Similarly, things which were rare or in short supply were very valuable to hunter gatherers, so phrases like 'only this week' and 'while stocks last' really trigger that fear response, and it is very hard to override.

A year or two ago I went to a stand-up gig by the comedian David O'Doherty. He went on a rant about how great the middle aisles in Lidl and Aldi are, where all sorts of miscellaneous tat can be bought for next to nothing. He talked about his excitement at buying a lawn mower from Lidl, knowing that there were only a few of each item issued and that he was lucky to get it. The punchline revealed that O'Doherty didn't even have a garden. Notice how you react to discounts and offers the next time you're shopping. Even if you don't act on it, there is an impulse to find out more. It's maddening, and it can be a serious source of clutter building up.

Stockpiling

A phrase I use frequently when shopping for food which makes Danny laugh is 'But then we'll *have* it.' It's what I say when I want to stockpile, something I love to do but have to limit because of space and money. Danny recently revealed that a gift idea he had for me was one of those giant bags of rice from the Asian supermarket, a purchase he has previously vetoed due to spatial restrictions in our tiny home. The fact that he knows me well enough to think of buying this for me filled me with joy and love (not to mention questions about my sanity and his life choices). Everything that I buy gets used, mind you. I also love the long-term financial savings of bulk buying and the savings on packaging. In my mad world, stockpiling is okay as long as the stuff is actually *used* and the turnover is high. We eat a huge amount of rice. It makes sense to me to have plenty of it.

During the Covid-19 crisis, stockpiling food and other supplies became rampant. I was amused by the scrambling for toilet paper, when no shortage had been predicted. I suppose when a crisis hits, the importance of everyday necessities of life becomes magnified. It's also, of course, about trying to find a sense of control when everything has fallen into chaos. Lisa Brateman, a New York City-based psychotherapist, explains: 'The thought to get milk before a storm is followed by the action or compulsion to go out and stockpile it. In one way or another, we spend a lot of time and energy trying to feel in control, and buying things you might throw out still gives the person a sense of control in an uncontrollable situation.'

From an evolutionary perspective, stockpiling and wanting to hoard resources makes sense. The person with the most stuff would have been a desirable mate and would, potentially, have survived longer. Now, for many of us lucky enough to live in wealthy countries, resources are no longer scarce; we can always go and buy more Sellotape, yet we want to keep three rolls just in case, all in different rooms of the house, and utterly unfindable when you need them.

Waste anxiety

Trauma and anxiety are now recognized as something inherited and passed down through generations. This fact can help explain generational anxiety around waste and scarcity. My father often quotes his mother, a Cork woman, who taught him that 'wilful waste makes woeful want'. My grandmother would have grown up in the turbulent interwar years and lived through the rations and restrictions of the Second World War, where frugality and using up every scrap were not only the norm but necessary for survival.

There is a very moving piece of art called *Waste Not* by Chinese artist Song Dong which explores different generational attitudes to holding on to stuff. The installation displays over ten thousand domestic objects formerly owned by Song's late mother, who refused to throw anything away if she could possibly reuse it. She had suffered poverty in the 1950s and '60s in China and had acquired a habit of thrift and re-use that led her to store domestic objects of all kinds in her tiny house in Beijing. After the death of her husband in 2002, her desire to hoard items became an obsession that began to affect her standard of living. Song and his sister managed to alleviate it by persuading their mother to let Song use her possessions as an art installation, reflecting her life and the modern history of China as experienced by one family. Photos of the piece can be found online and it's a pretty awesome sight.

I'm no sociologist, but I have a hunch this tendency is quite pronounced in Ireland, a country where not so long ago the general population grew up having very little, and where this time still clearly resides in living memory. As I mentioned in Chapter 1, many people call me on behalf of their elderly relatives, who have, for one reason or another, refused to start getting rid of their possessions. I never take on a client if the request doesn't come from them personally. I hope it is clear from reading this book that you have to be ready to do this yourself.

The notion that the traumas and triumphs of one generation can reverberate through successive ones is an old idea. It is not, however, a life sentence and it can be counteracted with understanding and compassion. If you struggle with getting rid of things because they seem useful, but you never use them, take some time to ask yourself how your parents treated their possessions and if you see any similarities. This can be a sensitive exercise, so please take care of yourself and allow yourself to process any difficult feelings that emerge through this exploration. Money and not having enough are very painful topics, so mind yourself.

Sentimental items

Danny has a pair of my shoes on the top shelf of his wardrobe. As I've mentioned, he is someone who cares very little for material things. Yet when I tried to dispose of my silver brogues which had holes and were uncleanable, he objected. 'You can't get rid of them!' he cried as he clutched the shoes to his chest. 'You wore these on our first date!' I laughed and left the shoes with him and they remain in our apartment, stored with other seldom-used items. Sentimental items can really trip us up while decluttering, which is why I firmly suggest they are the final items to be assessed. As I said previously, if you come across an old card or a treasured figurine, set it aside until the bulk of the decluttering is over. That stuff takes time to decide on and needs to be considered in a different emotional state.

For better or worse, objects we care about are the carriers of our memories. An item of zero monetary value like a letter can fill in the blanks in our image of a person who has long since passed away or an experience not thought of in years. Certain objects hold parts of our life story at an unconscious level. But a problem I frequently come across with my clients is a feeling of guilt about inherited items that they themselves have no emotional connection with. If you have items like this, take some time to properly unpack your feelings about them. How do we remember? How do we honour previous generations? These are complex questions, and the answer will be unique to each person and each item. I read an article by Vietnamese-American writer Thuy Dinh, who highlights this complexity while warning against Kondo-ing away the heritage of refugee families such as hers. She writes with sorrow about the loss of the family's traditional *ao dai* dresses, which her mother gave away in order to help herself feel more American. Dinh thinks that her mother would perhaps be surprised to learn that Dinh feels a sense of loss for items she has never even seen. On the other side of the coin, items are often passed on without retaining the quality that made them special, resulting in difficult decisions for future generations. As Dinh explains: 'Even if we decide to retain certain objects as keepsakes for future generations, there is no guarantee that our descendants will understand their significance. They need some memorializing context, especially if the objects in and of themselves "speak" nothing that can emit joy or excitement.'

As someone fascinated by material culture, I take these questions and complexities seriously. I know not everyone will be as nerdy as I am, but I think they are helpful to keep in mind when sorting through our own feelings about sentimental items, particularly those we've inherited,

Bringing these big questions back down to earth, my rule of thumb in terms of approaching sentimental items whilst decluttering is that if the item has genuine sentimental value for you (and take the time to be honest about this), then it is worth keeping and you can do so without guilt. As long as Danny doesn't start stockpiling my used toothbrushes, his love for my battered old shoes is valid. If someone finds that simply *everything* they own has sentimental value but they are still unhappy about the state of their homes, there may be an underlying anxiety problem, which I will address at the end of this chapter. For the rest of us, this is, frustratingly, very individual. What I *can* help with is how best to store memorabilia.

Storing memories

I am very careful about my box of letters, cards, scripts from college plays, photographs, memorabilia and, most importantly for me, my diaries. These items live in a plastic box in my wardrobe, safe from mould and damp. Over the years, I have slowly put some sense of order into the collection, both chronological and thematic, but this has taken time. I keep all my letters from my nan, for example, together in one labelled envelope, ready for when I want to re-read them. I used to be a divil for keeping every theatre ticket and cinema stub, but now I keep only the ones where the experience left a distinct impression on me.

Old-fashioned photo albums can take up a lot of space but are a practical way of preserving pictures. If space is an issue, I recommend removing any empty pages from an album if possible; many I come across are only half full. If you have a huge collection of family photos which lie in a disordered state and the task seems insurmountable, my advice is, as always, to do it bird by bird. Try and clear a space in your house that can be the photo sorting area so that the task can be accomplished over several days and weeks, if necessary. Aim to sort photos by categories such as:

- Events, e.g. birthdays, weddings, Christmas, and so on
- Chronology (if possible to gauge)
- Themes, e.g. family, work, holidays

Work out a system that makes sense for you, schedule breaks and allow time to process the emotions that may arise.

Scanning and digitally storing photos is often advocated by minimalists, but this solution presents many technical problems. Storage devices such as USB sticks or external hard drives do not last for ever. In fact, many only last five or six years, and after this there is a risk of the data being lost. If you wish to store photos in this way, the advice seems to be to update your devices regularly.

Cloud storage is another option, but it is often expensive and can expose your data to risks such as hacking or being wiped if your payment to the service provider fails, perhaps without your knowledge. I came across a useful podcast called *DIY Photo Organizing* which offers in-depth episodes on each of these issues. If you decide to go down the digital storage route for important sentimental material, I would recommend seeking expert advice on the best options to suit your needs.

Speaking of photos, large sentimental items can be difficult to decide on, especially if you are downsizing. Large framed photo collages or a once-loved collection of CDs can hold wonderful memories, but we may feel at a loss as to where to store them. A trick that has worked for several clients is to photograph larger items to preserve the memories whilst freeing up physical space. Again, seek proper advice about storing these photos long-term. I am often asked about what to do with old-fashioned inherited furniture that is no longer suitable for the owner's home. So many items will provoke an instinctual desire to keep them, so for anything we are unsure of it's important to interrogate our justifications for holding on to it. This can be done by writing out the pros and cons for keeping it, or simply talking it through with someone.

Gifts

A question I'm asked frequently is 'What do I do about unwanted gifts?' Before I answer that, I have to discuss our gift-buying behaviour, particularly surrounding the most clutter-generating time of the year: Christmas. I know, I know, I'm an absolute Scrooge, but bear with me. Every year, the shops fill with plastic reindeer that poop chocolate balls, grow-your-own-boyfriend kits and joke books about nuns getting up to mischief. These gifts are usually laughed at for approximately seven seconds and are then instantly transformed into clutter. I don't want to sound like the Grinch, and perhaps you know someone who would enjoy a pooping reindeer all year round, but somehow I doubt this is the case. It appears to have become cultural practice to buy and gift these items, and I so much want it to stop.

This stuff is landfill fodder. Show your loved ones or office mates a funny Christmas meme if you want to ease familial tension with a laugh, but please consider the long-term life of joke gifts. I would recommend a short film of the poem 'Boxing Day Blues' by Wilson Oryema (you can find it on Vimeo), which captures the emptiness felt after Christmas, when gift dissatisfaction sets in and the money wasted becomes glaringly obvious.

In happier news, I have witnessed a turning of the tide in recent years towards more mindful Christmas gifting practices; more people are buying experiences and non-material treats for their loved ones, and that's great. I'm not for one minute saying, 'Stop buying each other presents!', I'm just hoping that we can buy things for each other that have a bit more of a lifespan than the typical stocking fillers mentioned above.

Similarly, when buying presents at any time of year, think about choosing something that the person you are buying it for *might actually want*, or an experience like restaurant vouchers or theatre tickets. Think about whether or not the person is going to like and use the items, and try to get out of the habit of buying gifts for the sake of it. Frankly, don't be someone who dumps clutter on your friends. This sounds harsh, but I have to say it because, once gifts enter a home, they become shrouded in guilt and are nearly impossible to remove, like some sort of obligation limpet. I know it's hard and that some gift items simply must be kept for political reasons, to keep the peace. I remember having to attend Sunday dinner at the age of about ten wearing a comically ugly Christmas jumper my step-grandmother had given me (she is no longer with us so I can write this with impunity).

In terms of getting rid of gifted items a useful question to ask is 'Is this person likely to come to my home in the future?' It's an incredibly personal decision, and it's impossible for an outsider like me to understand the nuances in any particular family or friend group other than my own. As ever, be gentle with yourself and be honest about your needs if you can.

Cassie's story

Cassie was a young mum of three, and I could see the minute I walked through the door of her small house that she had a problem. There were toys everywhere, and I know that's normal for a family home, but I mean *everywhere*. There were tiny plastic creatures covering most of the floor, teddies and kids' magazines on every surface. This was another level. She took me into the kitchen and we sat down. 'So . . . talk to me,' I said gently. She was mortified but explained that she was separated from her children's father and that they both came from slightly chaotic but loving families of divorced parents, step-parents, step-siblings and foster siblings.

'Every time someone comes to visit or we go to see their cousins, the kids get showered in all this crap! I want it to stop, but I'm so scared of upsetting people. My mam has stopped giving them stuff because she can see the state of the house, but there are so many other gift bringers! I don't know what to do!'

We decluttered and tidied up the house, but I'm afraid I

had no lasting solution to her dilemma. Each family is unique, and I couldn't possibly have understood the different dynamics and tensions at play in her relationships. Nor could I tell her to forbid the children from accepting the gifts, as that would potentially cause unnecessary distress. I did advise her to try rotating the toys, a process I'll explain further in the next chapter. I share this story in the hope that it might strike a chord with someone who loves showering plastic on the children in their lives. Think of the parents, please!

Re-gifting

It can often be tempting to want to re-gift an item that was expensive or useful. This sounds great in theory but can lead to problems if not thought through fully. First of all, really think about the person for whom the item is intended. Is this something they *actually* want? Or are you just playing clutter Pass-the-Parcel? Some time ago, Danny convinced himself that he might have headlice (no idea why – he doesn't work with small children). Long after his headlice phobia abated, a bottle of headlice lotion remained in our bathroom and I became desperate to find it a good home – to the point that I brought it to a party where I knew there would be lots of young parents. Needless to say, I got some strange looks as I made my friends an offer they couldn't refuse (it turned out they could!). I share this cautionary tale to encourage you to avoid going overboard with the re-gifting.

Having said that, I derive huge satisfaction from gifting items to carefully chosen new homes. I recently gave a stack of drawing pads to a friend who is an artist and a collection of felt, gifted by a client, to a friend who is a primary-school teacher. Real joy can come from seeing your previously unwanted items find new and loving homes – see the end of *Toy Story 3* for a tear-jerking example. I experience this feeling most strongly when I attend clothing-swapping parties or Swap Shops, which are becoming increasingly popular. Seeing the old dresses that never fitted me right bringing someone else the buzz of having something new is really fantastic.

Saving things 'for good'

What are you storing away 'for good' in your life, and why? So many people in my life have items in their homes that are never touched, out of some strange idea that they are too good for use. During the Covid-19 lockdown, I encouraged people to enjoy everything in their homes. If you haven't yet done so, seize the day, friends! Light the fancy candles, wear your good shoes to brunch, use your most precious handbag every day. Enjoy your things! You certainly can't take them with you. Aside from not using them being wasteful, every time you deny yourself the use of the good bath salts or go for the cheap bottle instead of the expensive stuff that you're waiting to open for 'when you have guests over', you are sending yourself a signal that you are not good enough. Life really is too short, and you deserve to enjoy anything in your home that brings you joy. By all means save things for a special occasion if you actually intend to use them, but do not make this an excuse to hold on to items you will never use.

A note on hoarding

In this chapter about sticky items it seems appropriate to discuss the difficult issue of hoarding. The compulsion to hold on to items beyond all rational sense is a genuine disorder and one that I, frankly, do not feel qualified to help with. Hoarding manifests in a chronic anxiety concerning objects and was officially recognized as a nervous disorder by the Diagnostic and Statistical Manual for Mental Disorders in 2013. I've only ever had one client who I felt was beyond my help. She had kept every single piece of post she had received since the early 90s in their original envelopes, as well as boxes and boxes of empty medication packets. I felt completely useless when I left her, and all I could hope was that she would get the help she needed. For hoarders, objects can represent comfort and security. In the most extreme cases, hoarding is recognized as a medical disorder that can rob people of their quality of life. One study by researchers at Yale University used brain scans to show that for people with the disorder, throwing out objects activates a part of the brain that's also responsible for processing pain.[8] Hoarding can be a symptom of another mental health condition, such as Obsessive Compulsive Disorder or depression, but in other cases can be a condition in itself. The problem has become more widespread over the past few decades for numerous reasons, not least the availability of cheap goods and the increase in the average home size.

Once regarded solely as the subject matter of voyeuristic reality TV, hoarding is now thankfully being taken seriously as a health problem. Recently, in Northern Ireland, the company ClearOut became the country's first hoarding help service and is staffed by fully trained mental health professionals. I hope similar organizations emerge to help those struggling with this debilitating condition.

Final tips for sticky items

When divesting yourself of sticky items, remember that you're not just passing on physical objects, you're getting rid of the guilt that was attached to that unused item.

To commit to getting them out the door for good, I would offer the following advice:

- Have a designated area for items without a purpose, such as electrical leads you don't know the use for, Tupperware with no lid, solo shoes. Place these in a box with a label stating the date of their storage. If, the next time you discover the box, they are all still unused, out they should go.
- If items need to be fixed, place them in an easily reachable area near the front door and schedule a time to make the repair happen. Label them with the date, as above, and if a year passes and these objects are still untouched, please free yourself of

the guilt and recycle them. It is so easy for these items to fall into the background noise of our lives. Humans are highly adaptable and get used to new situations quickly; that's why a bag of stuff in the hall can initially look jarring but can very quickly blend into your home decor and re-enter the clutter stream if it isn't acted upon.

- Similarly, if you want to give an item to a particular person in your life, set a reminder to bring it the next time you know you'll be seeing them.

Conclusion

Sticky items really love to cling on for dear life. It may take some time and several deliberations over the same object before it leaves you in peace. Items peel away from our lives like onion skins, layer by layer, and it often takes a seemingly clear home to see the second layer of clutter that we had once deemed important. What we need, use and value changes over time. You may be surprised to find that an item you once thought you cared about very much no longer has a hold over you. This is normal and important to understand. Take your time and don't beat yourself up if you find layers of clutter weeks after you thought you were finished. This is a bird-by-bird process.

5

Kitchens, Bathrooms, Toys and Books

This chapter offers some to-the-point advice on specific areas of the home. Everyone will have their own individual horror areas but, as ever, be gentle with yourself and take it bird by bird.

Kitchen

'Capsule wardrobe' is a fashion buzz-phrase, but what about a capsule kitchen? Most houses I work in have kitchens bursting with crockery, cooking and baking equipment and glassware, not to mention non-perishable food that has long outstayed its welcome. I try to encourage my clients to keep only what they actually *use* in the kitchen. This makes daily cooking and the clean-up afterwards much simpler, as there will be far less rooting in drawers for implements and playing Jenga with plates and bowls in overstuffed cupboards. After years of living in cluttered house shares, I finally have a kitchen which is streamlined and user-friendly. 'Twas not always this way, however . . .

'Why do we have so many mugs?!'

Danny had a fair point. Our two-room apartment, occupied by two people, contained twenty mugs. Here's the thing: women like giving each other tea-drinking equipment. Most of the mugs in my collection are gifts, some of which feature pictures of my own mug/face (I have friends who like personalized presents). But a mug-provoked outburst from an otherwise reasonable man made me stop and assess. I gave away the mugs that did not have any sentimental value, and now we never worry about them all cracking into a pile of pottery because the cupboard is too full. I can already hear the screams of horror from two particular friends when they read this section. These individuals feel extremely strongly that different cups are required for different moods and beverages. If this is you, that's completely fine. But I bet there are still one or two you could get rid of.

What I strongly recommend when doing a kitchen clear-out is to bring everything that belongs in the kitchen into the same place. Go through the house, through all the school bags and lunchboxes, and bring everything to one sorting area. This eliminates a *Sophie's Choice* level of hysteria over whether or not to dispose of a topless piece of Tupperware that looks like it's seen its fair share of spaghetti Bolognese. If it's not in the pile, it's not turning up. Take a moment, shed a tear if you must, and either place it calmly in the recycling or use it for drawer storage, as I suggest below.

Treat glassware and crockery similarly to mugs. A cull is usually needed and will free up space in your cupboards.

If you're struggling with keeping your Tupperware and

other containers under control, I would strongly recommend storing these items with the lids *on*. This will save you from that common horror of opening the Tupperware cupboard and being showered in loose lids. If you have a fully matching collection and stacking boxes and lids separately makes sense to you, great. But in my experience, storing containers with lids on saves sanity. Even if it takes up more space, it's worth it.

Tea towels and fabric napkins are much better stored folded side by side rather than on top of each other. It's a storage change that I've really loved making. Any towels and napkins that have seen better days can be used as cleaning scraps or be recycled at a reputable textile bank (do some research: certain textile banks are fraudulent).

There is nothing more useless than a pot with a broken handle. Swear to repair or recycle anything like this. As I advise in Chapter 4, set yourself a deadline for repairing items and, if the date passes and the repair has not happened, admit to yourself that the item needs to go. Bring it to a tech recycling centre if you can.

Go through your food cupboards and throw out anything that is out of date. In the course of my work I have honestly come across food from the 1990s which should probably have been donated to science. Try and use this exercise to learn what you do and don't use so you won't waste money or food in the future.

With kitchen utensils, be ruthless. Do you really use that avocado cutter or the pizza slice, or was it an impulse purchase which now gathers dust in a drawer? Just because you have spent money on it doesn't mean it deserves space in your home. Remember the strategy for letting go of items which were expensive. Forgive yourself and set them free.

Junk drawers

Junk drawers are a physical manifestation of procrastination, a state with which I am worryingly familiar. It may seem impossible, but there is no need to have a junk drawer anywhere. As you slowly peel back the layers of things in your home, what you actually use and need will emerge. From there, you can store like with like, for example, batteries with electrics, paper with pens, and so on. I know it may sound like science fiction, but when everything has an obvious and easily accessible place in your home, nothing needs to be categorized as junk. I've already mentioned that having a bowl in each room to temporarily hold items without an obvious home is okay. But once the bowl gets full, it needs to be dealt with. I would avoid using a drawer for this purpose, as things out of sight fall out of mind and will get cosy and hard to shift. This is a system I use in my own home and it works pretty well.

'Put it in the attic' is not a decision

Question: What do the following areas have in common?

- Attic
- Garden shed

- Garden seomra/room
- Box room
- Spare room

Answer: They are all potential nesting places for clutter. Many of these areas stick out in otherwise organized homes as a personal Museum of Delayed Decision-making. Really, really, try to resist the urge to play Musical Chairs with your clutter. I was often guilty of storing my sticky items in my ever-patient parents' house. Eventually, once I moved in with Danny and actually wanted to build a proper home, I was forced to deal with items which I'd left in the 'storage unit' that was my childhood bedroom. It took some time, but over the course of a few months, bit by bit, I whittled it down to what I actually wanted to keep.

The most important thing to remember with extra space is: just because you have it doesn't mean it has to be used.

Paul's story

When I entered one client's house, everything seemed pretty normal. The typical possessions of a young family were everywhere, but I wouldn't have called the place *cluttered*. 'This doesn't look too bad!' I said cheerily. His face fell, and he said, 'I haven't shown you the attic yet.' Well. I've never seen anything like it; for a smallish attic, they had managed to cram in everything from old baby clothes to photo frames and broken furniture. It had reached a point of being dangerous. Everything seemed so finely balanced that I felt like, if I moved anything, the whole lot might come tumbling down. 'We just kept throwing stuff up there when we couldn't decide what else to do with it,' my poor client said, his hands over his face. 'It got out of hand.' This story ended happily, don't worry. We took our time and weeded through everything, transforming the attic into a useable space that was safe to walk around. Let this be a warning to all attic-dumpers: putting something in the attic or the shed is not a decision. It is setting up a merry-go-round of clutter. Really take the time to decide whether storing something you do not use is worth it. Your future self will thank you.

Bathroom

It may take some smelling salts to prepare you for delving into the unknown depths of a bathroom cupboard, particularly a deep one under the sink. Take a breath. It'll be worth it. If you genuinely benefit joyfully from having a bathroom full of products that you actually use, then good for you. For most people, however, their bathroom is a cave of expired medications and sun cream, ill-advised beauty purchases and half-used shampoo bottles. But it doesn't take long to clear a bathroom, and the feeling of relief can be huge.

Bathrooms can be another home for purchases bought with our aspirational selves in mind. As I've explained, we are often manipulated into buying things not because of the qualities of the product itself but because of the transformed version of ourselves it claims to offer. Make-up has never been something that has interested me, but I understand that it can be a source of creativity, joy and confidence for many people. The same goes for skincare routines and hair products. Try to gently assess whether or not your beauty purchases come from genuine delight or from an insecurity that should be addressed at a deeper level. I will talk more in Chapter 8 about the relationship between our appearance and why we buy things. It's something I continue to struggle with myself and is wired into us from such a young age, so forgive yourself if you feel conflicted about this.

To get started, take everything out of the cupboards. That way, you can see what you're dealing with.

- Group items together to make decisions easier. Hair products all together, medications all together, and so on. Useful products or medicines can then be stored together in one box or area. I use a shoe box for the medicines in my bathroom, with two smaller boxes inside it, one for plasters and bandages and one for tablets. The rest of the box is for creams and ointments and bottles of liquid medication. It works a treat and I know what I have at a glance instead of having to battle through sticky out-of-date bottles of cough syrup when I need a plaster. Out-of-date medicines and medications can be disposed of safely at a GP practice or in most pharmacies.

- Unopened personal-care products can be donated to certain women's shelters, but anything half used but no longer suitable will need to be disposed of. I would recommend washing out the bottle and recycling as best you can.
- Old make-up can become contaminated and should be disposed of similarly.
- Box storage is essential to keep order in a bathroom. Keeping similar items together will allow you to keep tabs on what you have and what's nearly running out, preventing unnecessary purchases which may become future forgotten-about clutter.

Books

Listen, I'll be honest, books are my clutter Kryptonite. My collection of poetry, novels, essays, memoirs, non-fiction and biographies is my most prized possession. I hold not one iota of shame or guilt for my bibliophilia. The titles tell the story of my life and how my interests have evolved and changed over the years. I'm also a huge re-reader and very much agree with Oscar Wilde, who said, 'If one cannot enjoy reading a book over and over again, there is no use in reading it at all.' For me, slowing my mind down by getting lost in a book has been such an important part of my mental health recovery that I despair at the suggestion that you might never re-read a book.

We live in a world where services like Blinkist allow us

to ingest books in a matter of minutes, breeding a culture of one-upmanship and a stuff-as-many-into-your-head-as-you-can attitude to books. It's that perfectionist 'I'm better than you' race that seems to follow us everywhere these days, a phenomenon we will delve into in Chapter 6. There are so many studies which prove that getting truly lost in a book positively affects our mental health. Turn your phone off and dust off a book you once loved. I bet you won't regret it.

We also all use books in different ways. I had a client who had a huge cookery-book collection. I commented that she must be a great cook, and she replied, a little sheepishly, 'I'm not, I actually just love reading them, they relax me.'

What I'm saying is that if books are important to you, never fear. I'm with you. I do, however, do a book cull myself every year or so and can offer help on streamlining your book collection if it's becoming a problem for you. Titles which can definitely go include:

- Out-of-date manuals and textbooks
- Bestselling novels or Man Booker winners from the early 2000s you bought and never read, and know you'll never read but keep out of some sort of intellectual guilt. Let. Them. Go.
- Out-of-date exercise and diet books. Ditch the Atkins and dump 'Pilates While You Cook', etc.

As an epilogue to this book section, a word in defence of Marie Kondo, who received a torrent of abuse when people misinterpreted her saying that she wanted each person only to possess a maximum of thirty books. I want to fight

Marie's corner by stating that she believes that if your books have value for you, then they can stay! She says on her Netflix show, 'For a shoe lover, it might be one hundred pairs of shoes, while a book lover might not need anything but books.'

The goal is to reach your own personal click-point, where you feel at ease with what you have. Reading a chapter of a book is also a great way to take a break during a decluttering session. Just saying.

Toys

Now, I mentioned that I do not have children of my own. There is no way I can understand the difficulties of keeping a home neat when there are tiny persons vying for your attention whilst making a mockery of any order you had put in place. I have had many clients with children, though, and here's what I've learned.

Toys are tricky, as children can become anxious about getting rid of their things. Preparing children for a clear-out can be very helpful. Last year I worked with a family whose two sons, aged seven and ten, were so fully prepared to help me work they were excited to see me when I arrived! On the flip side, I had a male client once who was thrilled to get rid of many of the toys in his children's playroom. I received a furious call from his wife that evening to say that he had got rid of things that the children loved and needed. This was a lesson for me, and a warning to you all! Be mindful of the other people who share your home.

It's obvious enough to advise you to assess your children's attachment to something before you suggest getting rid of it. But another layer to decluttering children's toys is that an adult may have an attachment to something that the child does not. Be aware of this and look after yourself whilst going through your children's things. If it's proving too emotional, take a break and maybe come back in twenty minutes after a refuel and a cry!

Rotating toys is a simple solution to an overflowing play area. Simply put some toys that are currently being ignored by little sir/madam away and take them out at a time when something new is needed. Several studies have shown that children can get overwhelmed if presented with too many options of things to play with anyway, so it's good for them too.[9] This can be useful to do at Christmas or birthdays, when lots of new stuff arrives into the house; just hide some of the presents and take them out gradually over the next few months. Several families I know operate like this, with great success.

Organizing toys can seem fruitless. They're no sooner neatly in a box than they're strewn across the floor/in the bath/down the loo (again, I don't have children, but I imagine that this is the vibe). You do not need to make your children's toys completely neat all the time. Large labels for boxes and baskets are really helpful, and you can get your children involved in making the labels too. Simply write words such as 'Lego' or 'Farm animals' and let them colour the label in. This makes the space theirs and not some draconian system you have imposed on them.

Kids' art

This is another tricky one. I had a client once who was an artist herself and couldn't bear to get rid of anything her children had touched with a crayon. We worked together to establish an archive for her three daughters, each with a separate section, using an old filing cabinet she had in the house. Weeding through the boxes and boxes she had kept took time, but it was important not to rush the process. In the end we condensed her collection to a manageable size. My advice with this is to display art when it arrives in the house, enjoy it, and then assess what you want to keep at the end of each school term. You can take pictures of any larger items such as projects or 3D pieces. Be mindful of what your children might want to keep themselves.

Sneaky items

Sneaky items are sticky items which appear to be useful but are in fact clutter. They also have a tendency to arrive in our homes seemingly without our consent. Things such as appliance manuals (all available online), out-of-date magazines, rogue socks we don't recognize and, of course, pens.

One of the great existential questions of our time is this: Where do pens come from? I have never knowingly bought a biro, yet they used to populate my desk drawers in what felt like an infestation. Pens are the opposite of socks: they don't vanish, they multiply. I have a memory of going to visit an aunt of my father's when I was a child. The aunt, at a loss about what to do with children, gave my siblings and me a large biscuit tin full of pens and some paper. This was a great way to occupy a group of bored children, but why did she have so many pens? Many other people I know have these boxes of pens in their homes. Why? At the risk of incurring the wrath of Big Pen, get rid of any that do not work (dismantle them and recycle any plastic parts) and use the pens you have before buying more.

Another bizarre habit that we have all collectively committed to is the hoarding of plastic bags under our sinks. Keep maybe six – ten at the most – and bin the rest. Plastic bags are not recyclable, even the bags for life. Get yourself a fold-up tote that you always have on you in case you stop off at the shops. At the very least, get into the habit of just binning the bags once you unpack your shopping. This sounds harsh, but it's where they'll end up eventually. Who are we fooling by squirrelling them away in this mad cultural practice?

Tips on how to end a day of decluttering

- Take photos of the bags of items which are leaving your home; this will remind you of your progress and keep you going.
- If you have the space, designate a drawer/basket/ area for items that are to be recycled or given to a charity shop so they all stay in one place. This can be where items which are no longer required can

be placed in the future too, ready to be grabbed as you head out the door.

• Following on from the above, schedule a time for charity/recycling drop-offs. Write it into your diary and stick to it. Don't let things languish in the boot of the car, or a hallway or on a landing. They can so easily creep back into the house like little gremlins!

Conclusion

Each room in your house will throw up its own challenges. The best approach is to take it one room at a time. Don't fall into the trap of leaving one room in a half-finished mess because you got fed up and embarked on another room instead. Children's stuff can be really tricky for some people, bathrooms can highlight our insecurities about our appearances, and kitchens can bring up that pesky scarcity anxiety. As ever, look after yourself, take breaks and remember why you're doing this. The peaceful and clutter-free home of your dreams is well within your reach. In the next chapter, we're going to zoom out from the minutiae of a personal declutter and look at the decluttering craze in its full context, as well as our culture of perfectionism and the shame it can provoke in us.

6

Decluttering is the New Black

We've learned how and why we have accumulated so much stuff and how to run a successful home clear-out. This chapter will explore why scores of Kondo-crazed households across the world are falling over themselves to rid their homes of joyless clutter.

Dr Joseph Ferrari, a professor of psychology who studies the causes of clutter and its impact on emotional well-being, defines clutter as 'an overabundance of possessions that collectively create chaotic and disorderly living spaces'. Google Ngram, which charts the use of certain words in book titles, shows that 'declutter' first came into use in the 1970s, and that its popularity shot up through the '80s, '90s and the first decade of the twenty-first century. Over the past few decades, more and more TV shows detailing the awfulness of living with a hoarding disorder have been cropping up on our screens. However, there was a gap in the market for helping ordinary families struggling with homes full of stuff and not knowing where to start. Right on cue, a smiling face with a perfect fringe landed in our midst, and no unfolded shirt or overflowing handbag has been safe since.

Marie Kondo

I have mentioned the phenomenon that is Marie Kondo already, but I would like to look at her work in a broader context. The huge response to her philosophy can tell us a lot about the state of the modern world. Kondo's much lauded KonMari method of decluttering involves questioning whether or not items 'spark joy' for us by holding them in our hands and reflecting on how they make us feel. Kondo also insists that we should show gratitude for items which are being disposed of by verbally thanking them for their service. Her techniques for folding clothing instead of hanging it in order to make the best use of a space has earned her fans from every corner of the globe. She is beautiful, immaculately dressed and accompanied by an equally lovely translator. She also seems genuinely kind and funny. I've read many, many decluttering tomes and so few of them actually mention her, but it is important to understand why she is so popular if we are to fully get to grips with our clutter problem. For me, the most important part of Kondo's message is the necessity for us to value our possessions with newly appreciative eyes. I'll talk about this more in Chapter 12. This wisdom has sadly become obscured by the sniggerings and cynicism about her cutesy vocabulary.

Marie Kondo wrote her first decluttering book in 2010. Sales were modest. After the devastating Japanese earthquake and tsunami in 2011, the book became a bestseller. Kondo's editor, Tomohiro Takahashi, explains that: 'The Japanese people suddenly had to ask themselves what was important in their lives. What was the true value of sentimental items? What was the meaning of the items they'd lost? What was the meaning of life?'

The same questions are now being asked by many around the world as we come to terms with the fall-out from the Covid-19 crisis, having already weathered a decade dominated by the consequences of the 2008 financial crash. During the coronavirus-induced lockdown, many millions of people across the globe were forced to spend much of their time at home, and I found the responses of my friends very interesting. Obviously, there was anxiety of many kinds, including existential, health-related, financial and social. But many people in my circle reported feeling more grateful for things which they had previously taken for granted, such as the food they were eating and the clothes they already owned. I write this whilst we are still in lockdown in Ireland, and it will be some time before the full effects of this crisis become visible. But it has definitely been a time to reflect, as the Japanese did in 2011. Questions like 'What do we truly value?', 'How can we reverse the pollution of our world?' and 'How can we find deeper meaning in our lives?' are not new, but have been asked in a new context during the Covid-19 crisis.

The craze for the clutter-free home

I'm obviously an advocate for decluttering your home. But I am also aware of the problems surrounding the current clutter craze. Being aware of the links between decluttering, so-called 'wellness' and our culture of perfectionism can help to strip away any societal conditioning about what you *think* your house should look like. Doing so will make your decluttering process more effective and satisfying long-term. Let's start with the global decluttering movement. It's not just Marie Kondo who wants to get her hands on our old broken plugs.

Kondo is certainly the break-out star of the decluttering arena, but her books are only one part of a global publishing and media frenzy for all things decluttered, organized and minimalist. Along with scores of decluttering books (including one by a Buddhist monk), there is a growing global minimalism movement. Several bestselling books have emerged about what is called 'Swedish Death Cleaning' (or, in plain English, 'Giving Your Things Away When You are Old'), a practice which has been part of the Quaker way of life for centuries. Mrs Hinch, Instagram star and now bestselling author, has amassed a gigantic online following simply for keeping her house impeccably clean. Films and TV shows like *The Minimalists* and *Tiny House Nation* are further proof that the material excesses of the past few decades are no longer cool and that minimalism and pared-back living are on trend. I wouldn't for one moment describe Kim Kardashian West as living a pared-back life, but I also think it's significant that she describes her palatially proportioned house as a 'minimal monastery'.

The core message of this book is that we *all* need to consume less, but I don't see the minimalism trend as a proper call to arms. On the surface, the fact that more and more people are participating in decluttering sounds like wonderful news for the planet and should be a major blow to marketers. However, as with most things, there's more than one side to the story. I want to take a closer look at how the declutter craze has become another route to self-optimization and, with that, another reason for many women to feel inadequate in a society which demands perfection.

Wellness culture, yoga . . . decluttering

A couple of years ago I came across an article in the political magazine *Jacobin*. As with all the best writing, it spoke to something I had felt for some time but could not fully articulate. 'Twenty-first Century Victorians' by Jason Tebbe describes how financially comfortable people in the Victorian era exhibited their wealth as a marker of moral superiority and that this is a practice we continue today. In the Victorian era, men displayed their wealth through the expensive clothing their wives wore, in the hope that they would appear not only wealthy but virtuous, that is, good. It was not simply that you were fashionable; your wealth implied that you were *morally* superior to someone, well, poorer than you. Today, although many people still buy into designer labels and luxury goods, the ultimate status symbol is glowing health or so-called 'wellness'. As the Jacobin article says, 'Yoga pants and running shoes display virtue just as clearly as the nineteenth-century wives' corseted dresses did.' The message of the wellness movement is essentially 'If I am healthier than you, fitter, thinner, more toned, more organic, drink more bee pollen smoothies, I am better than you.'

From the 1990s/2000s onwards, many of us have taken to displaying our 'goodness' by ostentatiously carrying a yoga mat into the office, humble-bragging about the organic vegan lasagne we've made or the juice cleanse we're on. I'm not suggesting that people wake up in the morning and think, 'I feel like displaying my class status and virtue today!' It's largely an unconscious process, but one many of us are vulnerable to.

The Victorians are infamous for their repressed approach to many aspects of life, from sex to parenting. We may have set ourselves free from some of their neuroses, but we *have* inherited their belief that an individual's moral credentials are based on their outward appearance, rather than their inner life. From this, we get those with unearned economic advantages looking down on, for example, parents who feed their children chicken nuggets, or patronizingly telling people who cannot afford the time or money for a yoga subscription that 'they really should look after their back'.

What's sneaky about the wellness trend is that the older, explicit consumerism of designer labels and huge houses was very clearly about money. Organic smoothies and expensive yoga retreats, on the other hand, are presented as #selfcare which every person ought to be able to achieve, rather than exclusive purchases attainable only by the rich. On the surface, there's a seemingly innocent desire to be healthy, but it's simply another way to say, 'I'm richer than you.' Think Gwyneth Paltrow with her increasingly outlandish health recommendations. It all boils down to an insane standard of perfection which women (and, increasingly, people of all genders) are expected to meet.

It is clear that the trend for neat wardrobes and sparkling homes is all part of the same perfectionism compulsion. Kondo and her fellow household optimizers have certainly sparked a craze. One look at the hashtag #konmari on Instagram will tell you how extreme some of the minimalism and organizing standards have become. I know that many people find it soothing to look at pictures of perfectly ordered homes, but does it really do us any good? Are we simply left dissatisfied by our own inevitably messy and imperfect lives? Linking food and exercise to good moral choices keeps millions of people trapped in the life-crippling grip of diet culture (more on this in Chapter 8), and now the pressure to make these 'correct' lifestyle choices has overflowed into the movement towards minimalism and an immaculately organized home.

While there is nothing wrong with wanting to be neater and more organized, a capsule wardrobe and obsessively ordered cupboards have become new status symbols. On top of that, decluttering and moving away from *stuff* has become the new 'good' thing to do. The psychology behind this is the same as the desire to walk into the office smugly clutching a green smoothie. It says, 'I've decluttered and I'm pure, and you cluttered folk are slovenly peasants who aren't worthy to kiss my carefully ordered shoes.' I sometimes refer to these pressures under the title 'lifestyle optimization'. To declutter with these motivations is not in fact changing our relationship with our stuff and our buying habits in a meaningful way. It is all about presenting a certain image of ourselves and not about getting to the root of the problem. If we can pare back the one-upmanship and the Keeping up with the Joneses nonsense of these lifestyle trends, then a genuine move away from wasteful consumerism can, hopefully, emerge.

The rise of the decluttering craze has coincided with the past decade of political, economic and social chaos. I see the trend for tidying as simply another means of numbing the rising anxiety we all feel about our lives and the increasingly chaotic state of the world. Political and economic turmoil are rife. Rogue viruses have the power to shut down the global economy. Record numbers of people are experiencing mental-health difficulties. We are drowning in stuff we don't need and never wanted in the first place. The trend for decluttering offers a small-scale, quick-fix solution to the increasing anxiety many of us experience on a daily basis. On a more personal level, let me explain how I came to use decluttering as a tool to manage anxiety.

Decluttering as anxiety management

On the desk in my apartment there's a Post-it on which I have scrawled, 'Decluttering is just a randomly positive by-product of my anxieties.' I showed it to Danny, and he laughed and said, 'You can't put that in the book!' I'm afraid, my dear, that I must.

A recurring scene throughout my teenage years and twenties was one of my parents entering my bedroom to find me sitting amongst a sea of my scattered possessions. 'You're at this again, I see?' they would say, shaking their mystified heads as they left me to it. I would pull out every drawer and every storage box and go through all my things in some sort of crazed organizational ritual. At the same time, I would rearrange my furniture. This was no mean feat, as my bedroom contained a lot of heavy wooden pieces, including a gigantic desk which wouldn't look out of place on the set of a period drama. Each scrap of paper, garment and trinket would be pored over and assessed for value, and then either discarded or rehomed. This was decluttering and organizing as anxiety management. I was trying to find a sense of control as my mind unravelled.

During years of rollercoaster mental health I got huge relief from being on my own in my bedroom, doing what I called 'pottering'. I can now see that what I was really doing was allowing myself to recharge from the world which so overwhelmed me, but I did not have this vocabulary at the time. I would go through all my things and try to find different storage solutions for everything. What I desired with this ritual was a sense that nothing was lost, nothing was undervalued or forgotten. The relief I experience when everything has been appraised and organized is still huge. We all find ways to cope with the stresses of life, and this just happens to be mine.

I'm not alone in using tidying and cleaning as a means of avoiding difficult emotions. Brené Brown, bestselling author and shame researcher, writes of a telling conversation with her therapist in her book *Daring Greatly*. The therapist asks, 'What do you do when you feel vulnerable?' and Brené answers: 'Clean the house. Eat peanut butter. Blame people. Make everything around me perfect. Control whatever I can – whatever's not nailed down.'

Mrs Hinch explains how cleaning has helped her manage her panic attacks: 'When you feel at your weakest, you're still achieving something.'

I have a friend who sometimes just needs to be alone and clean his kitchen to unwind his mind. This compulsion makes sense to me: control your external environment to calm your internal chaos.

Although my mental health is much easier to manage these days, I still love organizing and decluttering. No, I do not have Obsessive Compulsive Disorder; that is a serious condition, and I would never trivialize it. But the buzz I get from having things ordered provides what I see as a harmless stress relief, and I have been able to turn it into a business. I'm wired for it, as author Alain de Botton explained when he wrote: 'The more turbulent someone's inner life is, the more tidiness appeals . . . It isn't tidy minds that go for tidy exteriors, it's chaotic minds.'

In the broadest terms, decluttering is an outward expression of my deep wish for a clean and decluttered internal life. In my fantasy, I have a mind that is ironed out flat, neat and knowable. This wish is foolish and impossible, but I cling to it when life pulls me back under a wave of gloom. The mind cannot be decluttered. Thoughts cannot be filed neatly, emotions processed in orderly fashion when they arise. Our neuroses are not temporary but cyclical, returning from their orbit outside our consciousness when we are vulnerable. Accepting this is the biggest task for anyone who experiences emotional difficulties, which I would argue is basically everyone on earth. At this stage in my life, I am aware enough to know when I'm pottering harmlessly as a means to rest and when I'm in an anxiety state. I don't pathologize the organizing any more; it's my way of slowing down.

Perfectionism

We've talked a lot so far about making your home and your life better. But this task can seem never-ending in our current culture of perfection or bust. Many women, myself included, internalize the idea that anything less than perfect is a failure, and it's this troubling bind that we need to untie in order to break our decluttering projects free from sparkly Instagram accounts and aspirational (damaging) magazines. I am totally on board with that well-known maxim: perfect is the enemy of better. We have to look the beast of perfection straight in the eye in order to calm its toxic presence and to live our lives unburdened by unrealistic expectations.

Women feel the sting of wellness culture and lifestyle optimization particularly acutely. This is possibly because women are under such pressure in terms of their appearance and how they present themselves to the world in the first place, but also because, traditionally, women have been responsible for family nutrition and general health. When I was first thinking about writing this book, I told my editor I did not want to contribute to the 'You're Bad at being a Woman' genre. By this, I meant books telling you how to effortlessly whip up nutritious (but expensive and complicated) family meals, or beach-body workouts you can do on your commute, or whatever other nonsense they're peddling these days.

Brené Brown describes the modern woman's dilemma as: 'Be perfect, *but* don't make a fuss about it and don't take time away from anything, like your family or your partner or your work, to achieve your perfection. If you're really good, perfection should be easy.'

The pressures women face are real, and we can't opt out of them by choice because they are the water in which we swim. Many studies have found that perfectionism is on the rise amongst younger people. My fellow millennials and I don't exactly have a great reputation. We're often depicted as spoilt, entitled, lazy and financially reckless, with our clichéd avocado brunches. The reality is more nuanced. We grew up under neoliberalism, a system we didn't even know the name for as it took hold. We were taught that we were all special, unique individuals who could do whatever we set our minds to do. With the rise of social media, that message became even clearer: you are your own brand and your product is *you*. What we have internalized is that our value lies in what we can offer the market. That means never putting a foot wrong, for fear of losing social and professional currency. We are hyper-aware of what others think of us, and this causes feelings of shame and unworthiness, a sense of being overwhelmed by worry and a fear of criticism and failure.

I felt this very acutely as a young person. I was always *good*, and that meant I had to hide the parts of myself that seemed messy or shameful, even from myself. A book that blew my mind when I came across it was *The Curse of the Good Girl* by Rachel Simmons. It's basically the song 'Let It Go' from the world-conquering children's film *Frozen* in book form. Simmons writes about the pressure put on girls in many cultures to embrace a version of themselves which is unerringly compliant, 'nice', modest and selfless, and how badly this can limit a person's sense of self and potential. The idea of the 'good girl' is in fact so narrowly defined as to be almost unachievable. Some of my most interesting friends are recovering 'good girls' who learned to push back against this pressure and be themselves, warts and all. I would highly recommend Simmons's book to any women struggling with themselves. I think it should be essential reading for all parents and teachers too.

Shame

We are conditioned to believe that nothing but perfect will do, but what does 'perfect' actually mean? It doesn't exist. Yet we live in what Brené Brown describes as a culture of scarcity, or 'never enough'. We're never fit enough, never successful enough, never thoughtful enough, never attractive enough, never happy enough. When we feel that pang of not being enough, of not being perfect, what we are experiencing is shame. Brown has become an advocate for allowing shame to be acknowledged and faced in order to allow individuals to live more freely. After her fifteen years of research on the subject, she knows that this is not an emotion reserved for the mentally ill: 'We all have it. Shame is universal and one of the most primitive human emotions that we experience. The only people who don't experience shame lack the capacity for empathy and human connection.'

To put it plainly, guilt is what happens when we realize

we've done something bad; shame, on the other hand, arises when we believe that *we* ourselves are bad, instead of simply our actions. If I did badly in a college essay, I would see it as a reflection of my whole being, that *I* was wrong and bad, not simply the result itself. The same thing would happen if I upset or displeased someone, or if I had a clumsy social interaction. I was a perfectionist not in the clichéd way an interviewee might say it to get a job, but in a way that bred shame and became crippling.

Perfectionism is not the same as striving for excellence. It's the belief that if we do things perfectly and look perfect, we can minimize or avoid the pain of judgement and shame. It can be easy to think that striving towards perfection will make us happy, because we falsely believe it will protect us. The strangest part is that embracing our fear and shame, if done in a safe and supported way, can lead to a stronger sense of self. Trust me, I've been through this process and have read countless accounts of others doing the same.

These days, I try to operate from a philosophy of *good enough*. This is a famous phrase of child psychologist Donald Winnicott, who advises parents to give up the impossible goal of being perfect. I think we could all benefit from following this advice, not just with parenting, but also with our decluttering missions and in every aspect of life. We do not need homes that look like they have sprung from the pages of an interiors magazine. Homes are to be lived in, enjoyed, messed up – and who cares? They should be places of relaxation, not another rod to beat ourselves with. Now we have lived through the Covid-19 lockdown, we know this more keenly than ever. I would imagine that our attitudes to our homes have been changed for ever as a result of being stuck inside them for so long, but it is too soon to say what these changed attitudes may be.

If you are embarking upon any home or self-improvement projects, maybe think about ditching the lifestyle-optimization mindset and aim for good enough instead. Be grateful for what comes your way in life and do not be on the constant lookout for more. During the lockdown, amidst the existential anxiety and fear, much gratitude was expressed on social media for the simple things in life. I hope that mindset travels with us into the unknown future. We *are* wired to strive for more, it's what keeps us alive, but we have to find the balance between contentment with our lot in the present and hope for the future. As a therapist once taught me, the healthiest mental attitude you can adopt is: 'You're good enough as you are, and you can change if you want to.' Amen.

Conclusion

We've looked closely at the trend for decluttering as a life-style choice and delved into mental health, perfectionism and shame. These issues are at the forefront of so many people's minds, often without them even fully realizing it. It is very hard to detangle ourselves from the messages society is bombarding us with, but being aware of the problems is a good place to start. All this knowledge will be very useful for the next chapter, where we'll take on the decluttering minefield of wardrobes.

Part Three: Clothes! Clothes! Clothes!

7

Wardrobes, Women and Body Image

Wardrobes and clothing are such notorious sources of clutter and anxiety that I have devoted two chapters to this area. This first section concerns what I believe to be one of the root causes of wardrobe disorganization and indecision: women's anxieties about how they look. The strange phenomenon of people having bulging wardrobes but still feeling like they have 'nothing to wear' is due to many factors, including the massive increase in consumer choice, which I'll cover in later chapters. But 'nothing to wear' syndrome is also to do with identity, self-worth and body image. The next chapter explores decision-making around clothing and how to establish a clutter-free wardrobe. My hope is to teach you how to begin building a clothing collection that you truly love and that makes you feel good. This will reduce unnecessary future purchases and hopefully nurture a more sustainable attitude to the clothes we share our lives with. But first, let's take a hard look at why the diet, beauty and fashion industries have taught so many of us to hate our bodies in order to sell us products.

The thin ideal

You simply cannot talk about clothes without talking about bodies. In order to make long-lasting changes to how our fit-to-burst wardrobes are filled, we need to understand the links between clothing, diet culture and how women, and increasingly people of all genders, are manipulated into feeling bad about themselves so others can profit. This is essential groundwork for a healthier relationship between you and your wardrobe. Clothing relationship counselling, if you will. I've known what it is to waste valuable energy hating how I look, and I want to do what I can to help others free themselves from damaging mindsets.

Many women I know have a fraught relationship with their bodies and with food. Ads containing images of flawless models bombard us through our phones, our TVs and the magazines we read. Films and TV seem to give the impression that the only people allowed to be visible in the media are thin (not to mention largely white, heterosexual, and cis gender). In her influential book *The Beauty Myth*, author Naomi Wolf calls this uniform presentation of body type 'the official body'. She believes that the thin ideal developed as the grip of patriarchal ideas about male dominance began to loosen. Writing with passion and anger, she explains that 'A cultural fixation on female thinness is not an obsession about female beauty but an obsession about female obedience.'

Although we may believe that thinness has always been the preferred body type, fear of fat is, in fact, an idea rooted in racism, which has recently been co-opted by capitalism purely to sell products. The thin ideal is based on colonial ideas about black and brown people being inferior to white people, a belief that the world is still, tragically, grappling with. This is obviously a vast problem that I don't have space to fully explore in this book. I would recommend an article called 'The Bizarre and Racist History of the BMI' by the writer Your Fat Friend as a starting point for learning more.[10]

In more recent decades, these insidious ideas remain rooted in the world of commerce. It was during the 1920s that advertisers began to pick on something that was visible enough for women to be embarrassed about, difficult enough to change that it would require lots of products and, best of all, would never go away: fat. Whatever shape happens to be in fashion at any one time is a cultural preference. We hate our bodies for not fitting into a standard that is literally made up. Many fatphobic commentators will argue that we find thinner bodies more aesthetically pleasing because our hunter-gatherer brains register them as healthy. This is bogus and dangerous, but I know that it is a very difficult idea to unpick, because fat-phobia and connecting food and body size with morality is so ingrained in our society. Yes, there are some people who need to monitor their weight for health reasons, but the point I want to emphasize is this: you can never, *ever*, know *anything* about the state of someone's health based on the size or shape of their body. If you want proof, look up Ragen Chastain, an American health coach who holds the Guinness World Record for being the heaviest woman to run a marathon. Body diversity is normal, and if all of us ate the same food and

STUFF HAPPENS!

did the same exercise, we would all end up with different-looking bodies. And that needs to be celebrated and normalized. If you think what I'm saying is glamorizing unhealthy behaviour, then I would gently suggest that you seek out further information. I would recommend the dietitian Christy Harrison's book *Anti-Diet* and her podcast *Food Psych*, or the content of anonymous blogger and Instagrammer Your Fat Friend, who has taught me so much. Eating-disorder specialist Dr Jennifer Rollin and Health At Every Size (HAES) pioneers, such as Linda Bacon, have also done brilliant work in this area. I would highly recommend looking up an image of the Venus of Willendorf, an ancient figurine of a goddess. Marvel at her glorious stomach and round limbs. She is a powerful woman who was and should continue to be worshipped. The thin ideal is a fallacy, and it must be fought. Again, if any of this sounds mad to you, that's okay. These binary ideas of small bodies being 'good' and bigger bodies being 'bad' are, sadly, core societal values that are reinforced constantly, so questioning them can be uncomfortable. But investigating the reality has been hugely educational and freeing for me, and I hope it can be for you too.

I was very moved by a piece my fellow Irishwoman Megan Nolan wrote for *The New York Times* in 2019 titled 'Why Do We All Have to be Beautiful?' She describes the belief she learned growing up that 'to be beautiful was to have power over others'. I understood exactly what she meant. I would often tell myself that someone was arbitrarily better than me because she had a flat stomach or toned arms or better skin. It was that Victorian idea of appearances-as-virtue hitting me in the cruellest of ways. This compulsion – and I'd go so far as to say obligation – to be beautiful is also a patriarchal device. Women have been taught to place high value on their appearance because it largely kept them in their place. In more recent decades, the emphasis on women's appearance has prevailed for two main reasons: to sell products and to keep women as secondary citizens. Think of how much extra headspace women are required to dedicate to their appearance than men, from body-hair removal to anti-ageing measures to daily make-up. For many women, doing their make-up appears to be a choice which brings them much joy and empowerment. Make-up is also a creative and fun hobby, and a mindful and relaxing activity for so many people. But can you really *choose* to opt out of wearing make-up without bringing unwanted attention to yourself? I've been trying for years, with little success. I remember a friend laughing at me when I was a bridesmaid at another friend's wedding and was doing my own make-up. 'But Emma, you'll look *wrong* next to the others. You only ever wear a bit of mascara at best.' Yes, and that is my choice. But it doesn't feel like a very free one when comments like these appear so frequently.

Look, I know, it would actually be easier to go along with how women are largely expected to look. And I also totally understand the joy and creativity and confidence many people associate with make-up and grooming. I'm just saying that it should be a *choice*. I have succeeded in letting my eyebrows grow out naturally, which has been a big relief and time-saver. But I have a long way to go. These sentences are easy to type, but it is incredibly hard to remove these ideas from the deepest recesses of our minds.

Apart from make-up and grooming, the shape of our bodies is a huge source of anxiety for many, many people. I'm not going to go all Dove-ad on you and tell you to love your body. I certainly don't always love mine. Most of the time, I think I look fine. I did come to a life-changing realization recently. It has been creeping up on me for a while, but I am only now learning to embrace it and the happy freedom it has brought me. I realized that I will never be that tantalizing thing – *thin*.

It's such a loaded and cruel word, one that has haunted me since I was eleven years old and someone called me 'Emma the elephant' at summer camp. Throughout my twenties, the way I used to describe myself when I was feeling less than great was 'the hideous toad'. Getting older, being in a loving relationship and making peace with my relationships with food and exercise have all helped loosen the grip of *hideous toad* days. But I still feel sad when I think about all the hours I wasted thinking about my body, scrutinizing the parts I hated the most and wanting so badly to alter my appearance. Books, podcasts, TV shows (*Shrill* is essential viewing), therapy and carefully selected social media accounts have all helped free up my energy from the endless body-checking, pinching, pulling and self-loathing of the past.

I've come a long way from having to keep my coat on at parties because I couldn't bear the feeling of being in my body, and I'm really proud of myself and relieved at the progress I've made. Like the rest of my mental health, it's all cyclical, and ideas once planted can return at times of vulnerability. When I'm anxious or in a low mood, my body hatred returns, a lazy, well-worn thought pattern of self-sabotage. These patterns are deeply ingrained and aren't going anywhere fast. What matters is how we respond to them when they rear their ugly, cruel head. And part of that work is understanding where they come from in the first place.

Diet culture

'Diet culture' is the term used by activists to describe the widespread promotion of being thin and beautiful as the ultimate goal of femininity. It doesn't just mean 'being on a diet', because you don't have to follow any sort of official diet to be caught in a diet mentality. Even if you are not altering how you eat and exercise, if you find yourself repeatedly thinking, 'I'll do that/wear that/achieve that when I lose weight,' then you are living with a diet mentality that is probably costing you lots of valuable energy. By anti-diet dietitian Christy Harrison's definition, diet culture 'worships thinness and equates it to health and moral virtue, which means you can spend your whole life thinking you're irreparably broken just because you don't look like the impossibly thin ideal'. It's the idea that's used to sell everything from weight-loss tea (i.e. laxatives dressed up in a pink box) to luxury gym wear, snake-oil 'anti-cellulite' creams and eye-wateringly expensive and nutritionally suspect food supplements. All these messages about how we should look are near-impossible to escape. And they have a direct effect on our wardrobes, our shopping habits and our wallets.

Wellness diet

I've already mentioned the bee-pollen-smoothie-worshipping culture of wellness, which is simply a repackaged version of the ever-lucrative diet industry. When I was a teenager, at least all we had to aspire to was a Kate Moss heroin-chic thinness. Now, if women want to have the 'correct' body type, they are compelled to carve corsets out of their own bodies through gruelling gym regimes and disordered eating behaviours in order to be strong, not skinny (of course, this really means strong *and* skinny), with the perfect hourglass figure. Proponents of this dangerous trend for #fitspiration and #wellness will tell you, 'It's not about losing weight any more! It's about wellness! It's about health!' They're kidding themselves; it's the same thinspiration and fatphobia dressed up in another outfit. A wolf in Lycra sheep's leggings, if you will. It's still about altering your body to meet an impossible standard of supposed perfection, and it still perpetuates disordered eating patterns for so many of us as we struggle to stick to foods that are 'good' and avoid those that are 'bad'. It still equates a smaller body with moral superiority. The way many 'wellness' influencers talk on social media is eerily similar to the language used on the notorious Pro-Ana (pro-anorexic) websites, which encouraged young girls to starve themselves in the earlier days of the internet. The desired body shape may have changed, but the pressure to achieve it has only got worse.

This pressure is having a profound impact on our

mental health. In July 2019, the *Irish Times* reported that the EU agency Eurofound had discovered that young Irish women were suffering from the highest levels of depression in Europe. For Dr Cliona Loughnane, women's health coordinator at the National Women's Council of Ireland, the figures do not come as a surprise. She explained, 'The type of issues [young women] would bring up when they're talking to us is the impact of sexism in their lives; the pressure they face to conform; their ideas around a certain body image they have to meet.'

Several other experts quoted in the article cited pressures around body image as a core reason for the problem. This is alarming, and far more needs to be done to combat the dangers of our image-obsessed society.

Body positivity

The body-positivity movement has evolved online over the past few years in an attempt to combat the paralysing and sometimes deadly effects of diet culture. I say deadly, because anorexia nervosa has the highest mortality rate of any mental health condition, a fact I find shocking. Sadly, what began as a means for people with more diverse bodies to celebrate the way they look in a safe online space has been hijacked by the wellness industry. The hashtag #bodypositivity on Instagram now accompanies images of physical perfection as an ultimate goal, softened unconvincingly behind the thin veil of 'self-love'.

Body positivity may, sadly, have lost its integrity, but body liberation and body diversity are movements that I have found extremely liberating to learn about. Body liberation encourages individuals to cultivate a neutral attitude towards their bodies. It is less about loving your body and more about seeing yourself as worth far more than your appearance. This movement has helped me enormously. Not only has it helped ease the critical way I view my own body, but it has taught me to build a collection of clothing which fits me and makes me feel good. In the past, I would have discarded a garment if I saw a photo of myself wearing it and wasn't happy with how my body looked. This was wasteful and frustrating – I would love to still have some of those items. Nowadays, I try to remember that my body dysmorphia plays tricks on me and that if I feel good in a garment, I shouldn't be taken in by a badly angled photo. This isn't always easy; I have more than twenty years of bad body image to contend with. But I do my best to have self-compassion and to push back against the diet-culture messages whenever they re-enter my mind.

American writer Siri Hustvedt gave us the best description of body liberation I can think of in an essay entitled 'Outside the Mirror': 'Before I leave the house for an evening out, I check myself in the mirror for just a moment and then I go off, happily ignorant of what I look like when I am living my life.' I try to channel Siri whenever I walk out my door. She also offers wisdom on how warped our view of ourselves can be, even without a fully fledged body-dysmorphic disorder. In her novel *The Blazing World*, the main character, Harriet (Harry), says, 'I often wondered if I could truly see myself at all. One day I found myself all-right-looking and relatively slim (for me, that is) and the next day I saw a sagging, bulbous grotesque. How could one account for the change except with the thought that self-image is unreliable at best?'

How you *actually* look has little to do with how happy you are; it's how you *think* you look that counts. You don't feel self-conscious or unhappy because of the way your thighs, your face or your stomach look. You're unhappy because of the millions of messages that have been drilled into you that your thighs, face or stomach could have an effect on your happiness to begin with.

Now, to be clear, I am *not* saying that you are a fool if you care about how you look. I am not saying that you are a fool if you love exercise or eating well. All I'm suggesting is that we should all look at the motivations behind our beauty regimes and the roots of how we feel about our bodies.

Sizing

Diet culture has a direct effect on how we feel about our clothes. This can cause problems when decluttering for several reasons, one of which is our devotion to staying the same clothing size, no matter what. A little trick of the trade I learned when I was a costume designer was to cut the size labels off any clothes I was putting on an actor. This eliminated the possibility of someone getting upset if their trousers were a size twelve when they had told me they were a size ten. What mattered to me were the dimensions of the actual garment and the person who would be wearing it. I knew that the number on the tag was a ballpark figure at best. The British comedian Michael McIntyre has observed this stupidity, joking that in some shops his wife is a size eight and in others she is a twelve. 'If she's an eight, we'll have a lovely day together!', he explains. 'If she's a twelve, we have to go straight home.'

So it has been in my own clothing life. My wedding dress was a size 'S', whatever that means, but my jeans are currently a size sixteen. Even as I type that number a shiver of shame flows through me which I know is based on my faulty thinking about my own and other bodies. Why do I care what the number on my jeans says? It infuriates me. I had a crying fit in a shop when I had to buy size fourteen jeans for the first time. Danny was with me and could not understand why I was so distressed. As women, we are often told that our worth comes from a number, be that a clothing size or the weight on a scale. The actress Jameela Jamil started her extremely popular *I Weigh* movement based on her horror at seeing a photo of the Kardashian family containing each woman's weight floating above their heads. *I Weigh* encourages people to post a picture of themselves on social media surrounded by words describing them which have nothing to do with appearance or weight. A typical list of words accompanying an image might be:

- Good listener
- Survivor
- Loves drawing

- PhD Student
- Insomniac
- Good friend
- Dog lover
- Feminist
- LGBTQ+ ally

Follow @i_weigh on Instagram, or look it up online. It's a powerful and radical movement.

Clothing sizes are arbitrary and random. Some brands err on the size of small when choosing sizes, and some on the large. It's genuinely a free-for-all, and we cannot let it dictate how we feel about ourselves any more. Choose clothes that fit you, and cut out the tags if they upset you. Get rid of or store out of sight (more on this later) any clothes that you currently own that do not fit you, even if they appear to be the *right* size. Free yourself of the negative self-talk that comes from trying on clothing that doesn't fit. Life really is too short.

Danny told me that he wishes we could all see our naturally fluctuating weight the same way we do haircuts. We could say things like 'I've gone for a toned look this year' or, 'I've grown my belly out, it feels great!' and both these statements would be neutral and elicit neither praise nor judgement from anyone. What a beautiful dream. Hopefully, reading this section will bring you one step closer to that sweet freedom we all crave – the freedom to feel good enough, exactly as we are.

Tips on fighting diet culture

- Resist the urge to compliment people on weight loss. We have all done it, and meant well, but it implies that someone is of more value when they are smaller. Actually, it's best to resist the urge to comment on anyone's body, regardless of their appearance. We have no idea what's really going on in someone's life. I have a friend who lost a lot of weight due to crippling anxiety and got so sick of people telling her how great she looked. I have another friend who is thin and has been plagued her whole life by people worrying about her weight and assuming she's unwell. Keep complimenting people, of course; just steer clear of their size.
- Resist the urge to talk badly about your own body in front of others. Deborah Frances-White, author, comedian and presenter of the popular podcast *The Guilty Feminist* wrote, 'It is an act of internalised misogyny to hate our female bodies . . . every time we criticise our body, we objectify it and commodify ourselves. We make ourselves public property. This is a big problem for women as individuals and for feminism.'
- Try to develop the habit of noticing different ways in which we are manipulated into feeling bad about ourselves so that we will buy things. This is difficult, as diet culture and the thin ideal

are everywhere. It barely even matters whether we're aware of how images are filtered and Photoshopped: we still compare ourselves to them.

- The narrative around clothing that we have internalized is that if an item does not fit or suit you, your body is wrong for the clothes. Practise repeating the thought that it is the *clothes* that are wrong for your body, not the other way around.

- Intuitive eating is a potentially life-changing approach to how we feed ourselves that I would encourage you to seek out if you struggle with guilt around food. It is a process of making peace with food by getting back in touch with your natural hunger cues and your natural desires. Christy Harrison's book *Anti-Diet* is a great place to start.

- Though I have mentioned it already, I would really encourage you to find out more about the Health At Every Size (HAES) movement, which advocates for people in larger bodies and questions the instinct to judge someone's health based on their appearance.

- Learn to stop thinking about and talking about exercise as a way of compensating for eating. You do not have to exercise in order to earn permission to eat. This idea was even more rife during the Covid-19 lockdown, and it was awful to see. Unless you are an athlete, food and exercise should occupy different mental spaces in your head.

- Fill your social media feed with people of all shapes, sizes, and abilities, to normalize body diversity. Not just body-liberation influencers like @bodyposipanda and @yrfatfriend but celebrities who are changing the media landscape. My favourites are comedian Aidy Bryant, actor Beanie Feldstein, musician and all-round-queen Lizzo and, closer to home, journalist Louise McSharry, writer Bethany Rutter and model Curvy Nyome.
- You are not the problem. Your body is not the problem. The problem is the culture and the impossible ideal it promotes, not you. How you feel about your body is not your fault.

The clutter connection

These issues are directly linked to our clutter problems. Encouraging women to feel bad about themselves is big business. Advertisers know women's weaknesses for products which promise to make them feel even slightly more beautiful. 'Retail therapy' is touted as a harmless route to a quick pick-me-up, but shopping can often leave us feeling empty and dissatisfied if we are not simultaneously learning to heal the negative self-talk many people direct towards their appearance. We've learned to shop in the hope of achieving a shinier version of ourselves, as promised by advertisers. If we can learn to accept ourselves, I would hope that our clothing choices might become less aspirational, more considered, more sustainable, and more joyful.

Conclusion

Imagine if you didn't have to think about ways to shrink your body. Imagine if you didn't have to think up ways to alter your appearance. What would you do with all that headspace and time? Really think about it. There's a feminist fable of a patriarchy-free island full of fat, hairy, happy people of all gender expressions. Think of the outfits we'd wear if we didn't have to dress to show off our bodies. Think of all the 'flattering' but joyless clothes you'd banish from your wardrobe immediately. What a world it would be. In the next chapter, I'll go into specifics about managing our wardrobes and the many anxieties and tensions our clothing collections can represent. Getting to the bottom of these problems once and for all can point us in the right direction, towards a future where we no longer have to feel 'I have nothing to wear.'

8

'Is This Me?' and Making Decisions

This chapter contains tips on how to declutter your wardrobe for good, and how to store and maintain the clothes you love so that you can keep them for as long as possible. I have genuinely never had a female client who did not have a complex relationship with her clothing collection. I myself am no different. This may come as a surprise, but I absolutely love clothes and the self-expression and fun they offer us. Yet I still trip myself up with misguided purchases because of the complexity of the connection between clothing and identity. The fast-fashion business model, which I'll explore properly in Chapter 11, has a lot to answer for because of the speed with which new styles are offered to the consumer. There's a lot to cover, so take your time with all of this. Many of the blocks I describe below will have existed in your mind for many years. Even if you have never given a thought to fashion or how your clothing represents you, that in itself may be a mask for underlying anxieties. Not everyone cares about clothes, but I would wager it might be difficult to find someone who harbours no anxiety at all about how they look, even if they rarely think of these anxieties. They may be lurking at the back of your wardrobe. Be gentle and go slow if a wardrobe overhaul makes you anxious. I hope this chapter can help make the process a little easier.

Is this 'me'?

Our clothing is a big part of our identity. Even if you do not have much interest in clothes, what you choose to wear reflects how you feel and, like it or not, projects a message out to the world. We all have an enhanced sense of wellbeing and of who we are if we are wearing a piece of clothing that reinforces our sense of identity. This sounds great in theory. Unfortunately, what is more often the case is that women become confused about their clothing choices, especially in a world where they are expected to play many different roles. As writer Caitlin Moran explains, 'When a woman says, "I have nothing to wear!", what she really means is, "There's nothing here for who I'm supposed to be today."'

I've wasted so much money over the years on clothes that weren't suitable. It pains me to think about it, frankly. Why do some outfits feel like *me* and others do not? It's a strange phenomenon. When someone says, 'Oh, that's so you!' about something I'm wearing, I slightly panic. Who is the *me* to whom they are referring? If I don't particularly love the garment, what does their comment mean? This desire to have clothes that are 'so you' is, I think, part of the individualism we are taught to strive for nowadays. The fact that we say, '*Is* this me?', rather than 'Does this *represent* me?' is key. Clothing is inescapably fundamental to our sense of self, and yet many of us are extremely confused about what to wear.

Making decisions

In my experience, often there isn't a simple answer to the question 'Does it fit me and do I wear it?' which we can use to determine whether or not an item stays in a wardrobe. We learned in Chapter 4 about sticky items and the range of excuses we can concoct to justify keeping an unsuitable item. Here are several 'getting dressed' scenarios I have taken from my own life and the lives of clients and friends. Hopefully, they will shed some light on the complexities with which we are faced every time we open our wardrobe door.

- I try on the garment. It feels terrible. Perhaps it is itchy or too tight, or too big around the shoulders. But it was expensive. So I tell myself I'll wear it someday. I won't. It stays in the wardrobe, taunting me.
- The garment doesn't fit correctly. I tell myself I'll alter it. I don't. It stays in the wardrobe.
- The outfit fits, but I don't feel like myself in it. It suits the event I bought it for and so I wear it. I am uncomfortable at the event and can't quite figure out why.

- I try on an outfit that I once loved but which now feels strange on my body. I realize I've outgrown it but I cannot get rid of it for sentimental reasons. The garment remains in my day-to-day wardrobe, taking up space.
- The outfit is amazing. It looks so cool on the hanger. I put it on, but it looks frumpy and wrong. I feel like I can't live up to it.
- It fits, but I'm bored of it.

How can we free ourselves from these frustrating scenarios? By being systematically honest with ourselves about what fits and what works. This takes time and can be painful, but the benefits are huge. Finding a style of dress we are comfortable with and sticking to that can be liberating and allows us to know we will feel comfortable, no matter what we pick from our wardrobes on any given day. This does not work for everyone, however. I myself swing between wanting bright, colourful garments and wanting to only wear monochrome. These fluctuating self-expression ideas have confused and annoyed me for years, but now, with the wisdom of age and experience, I see it as a very natural desire for change and novelty. My clothing collection contains all the colours of the rainbow and I can pick and choose depending on my mood. Each person's wardrobe, taste and body image is unique, but the best advice I can give is to be fully honest with yourself about what makes you feel good and what doesn't and try to take it from there when making future purchases.

One really useful practical strategy for making clothing

decisions is to learn how to practise the body scan, a tip I learned from Annmaric O'Connor's book *The Happy Closet*. It's a variation on the spark joy exercise but with the clothes actually on your body. Pick an outfit that is a sticky item and wear it for a day or to an event. Pay attention to how you feel when wearing it. Are you uncomfortable? Are you constantly aware of your body because the garment is too tight or sits in an annoying way? Does it give you sweat stains? Can you sit down in it comfortably? Does that matter? This sometimes takes time, but you will feel so liberated when items are judged in this way. If you feel at all uncomfortable in the outfit but still can't let it go after reading the rest of this chapter, re-read what I've written about sticky items to help unpick your indecision.

Clothing categories

Various different aspects of your sense of self hang in your wardrobe, both in terms of who you are today, who you used to be and who you maybe wish you could be someday. Below is a list of clothing-specific sticky items which may be clogging up your closet.

Aspirational items

Certain clothing items are bought with an aspirational view of oneself in mind. Unfortunately, these purchases can often lead to feelings of inadequacy in the present, especially if they are glaring at you from your wardrobe each morning. I had a dress like this once. It was very sexy, tight, really not me – I don't know what I was thinking when I bought it. Yet I found it hard to part with because it took time to realize that I was never going to be that imaginary glamorous woman. And there was absolutely nothing wrong with that. Letting go of an aspirational item is not a defeat, it is a joyful act of self-acceptance!

Aspirational items can also have to do with weight-loss fantasies. In 2019 I had the pleasure of helping writer Hilary Fannin weed through her wardrobe, and she wrote about the experience in the *Irish Times*. She described how, as a child, she used to crouch on her mother's wardrobe floor and touch the soft fabric of the 'thin' clothes her mother kept hidden while she pursued endless weight-loss fads. Hilary explains that her mother's 'thin' clothes:

> were mostly unworn; they hung in the redolent dark solely to remind her of her weight-loss failure. A couple of nights after she died we found the diary she had begun that year, her 90th. Her entry for January 1st read: 'Lose Weight Now!' She did, in the end. We all will. The thing is, my mother wasn't particularly overweight. She was just on a lifelong search for a self she'd lost: a girl of 20, a 'slip of a thing'.

Let this story be a warning to us all; do not let weight loss rule your life, and banish clothes that make you feel like your body isn't the right size, here, now, today. This is simple to write and extraordinarily difficult to put into practice if you have been struggling with body-image issues. I hope that the body-liberation resources I suggested in Chapter 7 can spark the start of a move towards self-compassion and acceptance.

Discontinued selves

This is an academic term, but it often strikes a chord with clients as a way of understanding clothing which was once loved but no longer represents who they are. Maybe it's a style of skirt you wore constantly at one time, or some grungy jeans which no longer seem appropriate. Again, giving up these discontinued items does not have to be distressing, although you may feel emotional as you bid these vestiges of your former self farewell. See this process as a means of bidding goodbye to a particular stage of life with gratitude.

Sentimental items

I've already told you the story about Danny keeping my silver brogues. Clothing is very emotional for many people. Sentimental clothing such as first-date dresses, your mother's cardigans, college T-shirts, and so on, should not be stored with everyday clothing. These items can be permanently stored in a separate box or drawer, if one is available. Use mothballs and wrap the items in white tissue paper if possible, to avoid them catching on each other. Coloured tissue may bleed over time, so avoid using it. I was astonished recently by the emotions I experienced when I unearthed an old jumper of Danny's. What appears to be washed out and no longer fit for use is a treasure to me that I will keep for ever. Many garments contain the stories of our lives and should be cherished accordingly. But don't start playing the sentimental card to justify keeping items for other reasons. Be honest with yourself and the true value of an item will emerge.

Clothing that's 'fine'

A friend of mine asked me to write about those strange grey-area clothes that we hold on to for when we're premenstrual, depressed or exhausted, when life is neither good nor bad but somewhere in between. These clothes are a part of most people's wardrobes, and as long as they're not clogging up too much space, they have a right to be there. I'm not saying keep every last ratty T-shirt, but one or two pairs of washed-out sweatpants and a hoodie are okay as long as they serve a particular purpose and are actually worn.

Many of us also need clothing that is plain and practical for our work. Of course, it would be wonderful to feel fantastic in everything you own, and I would encourage you to seek work clothing that makes you feel confident. It does take a little bit more effort, but it will help you value your clothes and keep them in use for longer, instead of treating workwear as disposable because it does not 'spark joy'. In practical terms, however, most of us will need garments that we don't necessarily love. When assessing these items for culling or keeping, ask yourself if you're keeping too many 'handy' garments and see if you can allow yourself to buy workwear that you actually love and which will last you a long time. I had a client who worked in a bank and who wore black clothing five days a week. When we were going through her wardrobe, she was astonished by how many black shirts she had, some of which she had never worn. 'I guess I just pick them up when I see them,' she explained, staring at the huge pile on her bed. 'I barely think about it.' We weeded out the shirts that she didn't like and, reeling from our discoveries, she ended the day intending to be much more mindful when buying work clothes.

Gifts and hand-me-downs

One client had a large number of items in her wardrobe that were gifts from her sister but which she had never worn. We slowly and carefully assessed each garment and realized that none of them actually suited her but that she had accepted them because they were *good quality*. By the end of the session she had sworn never to accept a clothing gift from her sister again (in the most diplomatic way possible, of course). I used to do this all the time, both when I was a costume designer and when I decluttered for friends. Be really careful what you bring into the house. It's much harder to shift it once it's found a home and appears to have earned its place. Practise saying a gentle 'no' when cast-offs are offered that won't suit.

Event items

Event items have become a large source of textile waste. In a recent study by the charity Barnardo's, a quarter of those questioned said they would be embarrassed to wear an outfit to a special occasion such as a wedding more than once. This rose to 37 per cent of young people aged sixteen to twenty-four but just 12 per cent of those over fifty-five. We really need to buck this trend. At my own wedding, many of my friends who know how I feel about wasteful purchases made a point of re-wearing dresses or suits that they already owned. I was thrilled, but the fact that these were noteworthy decisions spoke to the ridiculous belief that being seen in the same outfit twice is somehow bad. You can always re-style a much-loved dress with different shoes, bags, jewellery or even by changing your hair and make-up (if that's something you're into).

Occasion wear can also be a source of confusing clutter. A friend of mine loves holding on to frumpy clothes she never wears with the excuse that they are 'handy for weddings'. She also loves holding on to garments for even more specific occasions, so much so that it has become a joke between us:

OMG, I *have* to keep this weird shapeless jacket I've never worn! What if I have to attend a colleague's child's chris-tening on a boat?!

Or:

This nylon lime-green dress would be perfect for my accountant's retirement party!

If this is you, try to be as honest with yourself as pos-sible. Try a body scan, and if the item really doesn't work, bid it farewell with a sigh of relief and gratitude.

Summer clothes

Summer clothes are a serious source of household waste. The Barnardo's survey found that in the UK people spent £2.7 billion in 2019 on more than 50 million summer outfits that will be worn only once. By far the biggest extravagance is new clothing for holidays, where consumers splash out more than £700 million on 11 million items bought for one trip which will never be worn again. This is bananas! I accept the findings that more than half (51 per cent) of those surveyed said buying new clothes for a festival or holiday added to the excitement of the build-up, but surely those items could then be kept and reworn on subsequent holidays? To avoid the typical Penneys/H&M splurge on cheap and disposable holiday wear, try borrowing a bag of summer clothes from a friend who's your size. The clothes will feel new to you and you'll get that novelty hit without feeding the fast-fashion monster.

Categorizing items as 'summer clothes' is often used as an excuse to keep unsuitable garments. 'I'll wear it on holiday!' you say, folding away the shapeless dress. Trust me, it'll still be ugly in Spain. Try not to fall into this trap and, again, be honest about what you will or won't wear.

Summer clothing should be stored separately from everyday wear. Make sure it is washed before storing as this will stop odours from building up over time. In Ireland and the UK, of course, 'summer clothes' used to mean the few items we had to take on holidays. The climate crisis and the accompanying rise in summer temperatures has meant that we use these summer garments more frequently. Let's treat them as we would any other item in our wardrobe, with love and care and the intention to keep them long-term.

Hibernating

No, this section is not a wildly irrelevant digression about hedgehogs, but a method for making the harder clothing decisions easier. For items that you're not sure about, like a dress that needs altering or trousers that never quite look right but which you love, place these sticky garments in a drawer or box and put a note in your diary to reassess them in six months' time. I would strongly advise you to do this with anything in your wardrobe that makes you feel like your body isn't the size it's meant to be right now. Even if you are intending to lose weight or have just had children, for example, store the clothes that don't fit you out of sight.

This process helped a friend of mine recently. She had a box full of jewellery that was broken and which she'd been planning to fix. I asked her to promise me that if they were still there in a year's time, unfixed, she would part with them. She was sceptical about my suggestion at the time, but when we found the box a year later she realized that she was never going to fix them and felt much better about letting them go.

Loved clothes last

If you love what's in your wardrobe, you will buy less and stay clutter-free. Everyone (I hope) has at least a few items in their wardrobe that they love and which they plan to keep long-term. The outfit I chose for my wedding was a simple summer dress that I adored and in which I felt completely comfortable. I wore it twice on my honeymoon and when I posted about this on Instagram I received a shower of positive feedback. One friend, whose parents run a vintage clothing business, wrote:

> Clothes have so much more life when you can describe where you found them, what they've lived through. They earn their own moods – one thing is worn when you feel like standing out, and another when you feel like you need its warm comfort. Re-wearing and mending beautiful clothes is just like keeping a fantastic memory book.

Another person commented:

> Many of my favourite clothes I have had for decades. For me, their charm never dims. Like a much-loved re-read book, the fabric carries the patina of my life. A dress without provenance is merely another dull rag hanging in a department store.

These items are washed with care, repaired when needed and generally treated with the respect that all clothing deserves. If we can harness this level of care for more of our wardrobe, we will reduce our desire for new stuff and be happier with what we have into the bargain. This is the philosophy of one of my heroes, Kate Fletcher, and is the cornerstone of her project The Craft of Use, which encourages us all to place higher value on our clothing collections. She asks the radical question, 'What if we paid more attention to the tending and wearing of garments than to their acquisition?' Fletcher hopes to change the fashion industry by slowing down the incessant churn of disposable pieces and to help us learn to view our clothing in a different way. I believe that there is a promising appetite for this, based on the current enthusiasm for sustainable fashion in younger generations and many older people's irritation with low-quality garments.

If we can learn to value our clothes in a different way, we can gradually discover what we actually like wearing and therefore be equipped to make more conscious decisions when shopping for clothes. I don't always meet these standards myself, and still make clothing decisions that I regret, but my aim is to love and care for everything I own equally, including my clothes. I participated in Fletcher's Local Wisdom project back in 2013. This part of her research involved interviewing members of the public about an item of clothing which had a story behind it. I chose the top half of an old pair of my dad's paisley pyjamas and a dress I have had since I was in school and which I've worn everywhere from the beach to a formal college dinner. I still have it. Take a look in your wardrobe and see what items have stories behind them. And the next time you're shopping, maybe ask yourself whether something you want to buy will really add to your life, will enrich your clothing story. Of course, I understand that sometimes you just have to buy jeans or a new top for work, but it's a habit I would encourage you all to gradually adopt.

Looking after your clothes

If you love what you own, you will also be more likely to look after your clothes and repair them, and I guarantee you will feel happier and more confident overall. Looking after your clothes takes a small bit of effort, but the gains are big. Get your shoes re-heeled at a good cobbler's. If you have suede boots, buy a brush for them to keep them in good nick. Debobble your jumpers and coats to make them like new again and, for goodness', sake, learn how to sew on a button! It's a skill that should be compulsory for all secondary-school students of all genders. Looking after our things helps us connect with them and gradually move away from seeing clothes as disposable.

Many of us have got into the habit of washing clothing unnecessarily. Over-washing damages garments, and it can be heartbreaking when a much-loved item is washed out of existence. Hand-washing clothing is nowhere near as painful as it sounds, particularly with amazing products out there like Soak, which does not require rinsing. Danny initially thought I was disgusting for suggesting that he wash his clothes less, but he now hand-washes his shirts and jumpers and can't believe how much longer they last as a result. Even low-quality items can be maintained for longer if they are treated with the same care as more expensive garments. The problem is that when clothes are cheap, we think nothing of throwing them into a hot washing machine and then disposing of them if they shrink. Treating all textiles with care, regardless of their original monetary value, will contribute to our wardrobes being more consistent, less wasteful and more satisfying. Always use your garment tags as a guideline when washing them; they are easily forgotten about, especially with cheaper items, but if followed properly they will prolong the life of the garment.

There are numerous ways to refresh clothing that has only been gently worn.

- Instead of shoving items that don't need immediate washing, like jumpers or jeans, in a drawer, hang them up so that air can circulate to refresh them.
- If a garment gets a small bit of food or dirt on it, simply clean that one area by hand instead of putting the clothing into the laundry basket. This will save that item from an unnecessary trip to the washing machine, as repeated machine-washing wears down fabric over time.
- You can also clean garments that are not dirty and have only been gently worn by hanging them up in the bathroom while you take a shower. The steam from the shower gently removes odours from fabric. This really works! (Don't do this for items that are dry-clean only.)

- A trick used in the costume trade is to spray items that are difficult to wash with vodka. You read that right: vodka. The alcohol helps kill germs and neutralize odours with no damage to the fabric. All fabrics are suitable for this, except for those pesky dry-clean-only items. This hack obviously often gives rise to jokes being made about why a costume budget often contains three litres of vodka. 'It's for cleaning, we swear!', the costume team would say, winking at each other.

- One last hack, and possibly the craziest, is to put garments in the freezer to kill odours and bacteria. I promise you, I have done all of these things, and they really work. I know it may seem eccentric, but so did recycling, once upon a time. We need to change our mindsets from our current cleaning addiction to a more gentle way of caring for our clothes.

Wardrobe curation

We can grow visually tired of what we see every day, taking for granted the clothes we once loved. This is also the reason bags of clutter can build up in our homes almost imperceptibly; we get used to seeing them and they no longer seem urgent, until we reach the tipping point and choose to start getting to grips with our stuff. In terms of our clothes, there is an easy way to get round this problem – wardrobe curation. 'Curation' is a word usually associated with museum collections. For me, curating my clothes has become a habit which allows me to fully appreciate everything in my wardrobe. The process is simple: after decluttering the wardrobe fully, store a small number of items out of sight temporarily, in under-bed storage or similar. Take this selection out when you're feeling tired of what's in your wardrobe and you instantly feel like you have a rake of new things! Rinse and repeat.

This trick only works on items that are not flash-in-the-pan trends. But if what's in fashion is important to you, curating can also help get you in touch with the fact that so much of fashion is cyclical. A velvet dress you love, or your favourite flared jeans, may go out of style, but they will definitely be *in* again in a few years. Fast fashion can make us forget this fact, because style change is so accelerated, but everything really does come back around. Well, except maybe the worst of the '80s trends.

If your problem is always needing the latest things and feeling compelled to shop for clothes, I would recommend the book *The Happy Closet* by Annmarie O'Connor. It's a light-hearted guide to kicking compulsive shopping and gaining control over your clothing choices. She suggests a useful experiment called the 10 Kilo Challenge, which involves filling no more than a small suitcase (approx. 10 kilos) of clothing and wearing only the contents of the bag for two weeks. It's a great way of appreciating your clothes and seeing what in your wardrobe actually works for your day-to-day life.

Wardrobe storage tips

- Use the same style of hangers for everything, if you can; your wardrobe will look neater that way.
- Hooks on the inside of a wardrobe door are the best solution I've found to the fiddly problem of jewellery storage. I hate those stupid mini-mannequins that are supposedly for necklaces. Everything gets so tangled and you can only use what's at the top – they are a pest! Unless they are of sentimental or aesthetic value, please bid them farewell. You want to be able to actually choose what jewellery you wear without having to go to war with a tangle of beads.
- For earrings, a large Ferrero Rocher box can work a treat! I know this wouldn't be for everyone, so my advice is to source a storage tray with multiple small compartments and so eliminate the risk of cross-contamination. For studs, I have a piece of foam into which I stick the earrings, and I store the backs in a small box beside it.
- Divide your drawers. You don't need fancy storage solutions. Settle for using whatever boxes you have to hand to keep your bras away from your socks and your gym wear separate from your jeans. Store like with like, as best you can, and you can't go wrong.

- I roll my tights and keep them in a cardboard box, one for black, one for navy and one for anything else. This works well, as I was forever putting on the wrong colour of tights and only realizing when I was out in the world and it was simply too late. Not ideal.

Conclusion

Wardrobes are the most dreaded decluttering project for many people. All the more reason to change our shopping habits, learn to look after and love our clothes, and stop the clutter building up again. Really take your time with this: our ideas about how we look, what we should wear and how we should shop are deep-rooted and can only be shifted with effort and patience. Remember: this work is not a crash diet, it's (hopefully) a long-term habit change. As we've learned, there is much work to be done to adjust how we value our clothes and the bodies that wear them. But I have offered some food for thought and simple hacks which will, I hope, contribute to a healthier and more loved wardrobe, a healthier outlook on body image, and a few tips for how to start buying clothes in a more satisfying way.

Part Four:
Organization

9

Finding a System that Works for You

Organizing and deciding how to store items should only be attempted after a ruthless and honest purge of stuff. The next step is to keep items that are connected by use and type together and store them in a place which is accessible and practical so that they can be used and enjoyed. This step is key to staying clutter-free long-term. I have given you lots of storage tips along the way, but in this chapter I want to dig into some of the broader ideas about how to approach organizing your home. This is the part of the process I love the most. It really gives me a kick to see the proper flow of a room or house coming together. Nothing hidden or forgotten and nothing useless or ugly. The dream.

House flow

House flow may sound like a new style of music only the cool kids listen to, but it is in fact a design term which refers to how the furniture and storage is laid out in your home. I would extend this definition to include the flow of how your possessions go from storage, to being in use, to storage again. I mentioned clutter hotspots in Chapter 2. These can build up at the points where the flow of a room breaks down, causing stress, mess and time-wasting. That is why, after a declutter, it's really important that you don't immediately put all the items that you are keeping back where they originally were. Take some time to see if you need to rearrange your furniture to help prevent clutter hotspots from returning. I would recommend Laura de Barra's book *Gaff Goddess* for more tips on this. Also take the time to ask yourself if, for example, your jeans might be more accessible in a different drawer, or if the saucepans are stored in an annoyingly high cupboard. Could you change things to make your life easier? It's like moving house in your own home! You get to start from scratch. It's a joy. It's far more important to have a set-up that's easy to manage than one that looks picture perfect after a one-off declutter but is chaos the rest of the time. When deciding how to better organize the storage of your possessions, my advice is to ask yourself the following questions:

- What do I use every day?
- Are those items easily accessible?
- How can I make those items as easy as possible to tidy away after use?

The flow of things that you use in your home can seem immovable, but we are adaptable creatures. New systems can be adopted pretty quickly, as long as the system works for all the organizational personalities sharing your home.

Personal organizing style

We are all familiar with the images of perfectly organized wardrobes or kitchens which float around the internet. But how neat an area looks after a one-off tidy means very little after the momentary glow of satisfaction wears off. What matters is the *system* you set up for organizing your things long-term, and how sustainable that is. The question to ask is not 'How can I make my wardrobe look neat?', but 'How easy is it to put things away in my new system?' Being able to put things away easily is so, so important. It really is the make-or-break factor in whether or not a room remains neat longer than a couple of days after a declutter. But what's essential to understand is that not everyone sees organization in the same way.

Naomi's story

In the early days of my decluttering business I had a client who loved storage solutions. Each room of her house was full of labelled boxes and plastic stacks of drawers, each full to the brim with stationery, toiletries or electrical bits and bobs. Yet there was still stuff *everywhere*. Every surface was covered in books, toys, paperwork and clothes. So far, so typical. We decluttered, removed anything unwanted from the house, and I felt satisfied when I left her. Six months later she called me again. The house was back the way it was, chaotic and unmanageable. I couldn't really understand this, and neither could she. I told her I would investigate different storage solutions and discovered an essential principle of decluttering; not everyone organizes in the same way. This particular person had set up complicated micro-storage for herself with very specific categories for things like types of batteries, paperwork and children's art. What we eventually figured out suited her better was a macro system, whereby everything is organized in broader categories. One example was that we bought a large box for her children's art to replace the barely used filing box in which she had intended to place their work by age and even season. This made it far easier to tidy away the art instead of leaving it lying around because she didn't have the natural inclination or desire to file it away. With my help, she also realized that the paperwork in her neat desk inbox tray never got dealt with. This was because she was a visual person and had to *see* papers that needed to be acted on. The solution was a large message board with magnets onto which her to-dos were stuck. This allowed her to feel calm and more in control of her house and life.

Before you start this process, it is essential that you pinpoint and understand your own personal organizational style. Some people want all their possessions visible because that is how they remember to use them; others want things hidden but neatly ordered. According to Cassandra Aarssen, author of the brilliant organization guide *The Clutter Connection*, there are four main categories of organizing style:

- Possessions mostly visible on shelves and in containers with *macro*-organization, that is, within broad categories like 'Batteries', 'Greeting Cards' or 'Art Supplies'

- Possessions mostly visible with *micro*-organization, that is, very specific categorization of objects (an example might be having different boxes for different sizes of battery instead of all batteries in one box)
- Possessions largely hidden in drawers, cupboards and wardrobes, grouped together in broad macro-categories
- Possessions largely hidden, grouped together into more specific micro-categories

As I said at the start of the book, none of us fits neatly into boxes of personality and behaviour. I offer these ways of organizing as broad suggestions. You might fall into two of these and, indeed, your preferences may differ from room to room. I am broadly visually minded and macro-orientated when it comes to my wardrobe; this means I do not colour-code my knickers or need all my shirts facing a certain way. Yet I am micro when it comes to my stationery, wanting my desk drawer to be divided neatly into categories and for my pens to be separate from my Post-its. A friend of mine, a cooking enthusiast, likes the kitchen to be neat when he is working and organizes his equipment obsessively. Yet his bedroom is strewn with papers and odd socks. We are all perfectly unique in our household habits, so this lesson about flexibility in approaching organization is crucial. It might save you a good bit of hair-pulling and hand-wringing to know that workable, neat alternatives exist to images of home storage you might have seen on Pinterest or Instagram.

Take some time to observe your home and figure out what works for you. Do you need the post that requires attention in full view in case you forget about it? Or do you prefer to put it in a file marked 'to-do' or similar? Do you want all your clothes colour-coded? Or do you simply want the clean separated from the dirty? Defining your own organizational style is particularly useful for people who believe themselves to be naturally messy. This is not the case! It is simply that the idealized organization image of a bare room with neatly labelled boxes and shelves hidden away is only one way of organizing.

For long-term success, try to get everyone who will be using a space to contribute to its design so as to give them some sense of ownership and not make them feel like they are simply carrying out the instructions of the organizing overlord. This might also help share the emotional labour of devising and maintaining these systems. A clash of organizing styles can cause tension within the home. Unfortunately, if you desire an Insta-perfect micro-organized paradise but your family members can only manage broader organization, then you will have to defer to their way of thinking. This is the only way your home will remain in any way neat.

Macro-organizing systems can mean that slightly more time (a few seconds) is needed to find an item. What is crucial is that, for people with macro-orientated minds, a system like this makes *putting things away* totally simple. And that really is key. Everything must have a place, so that you can easily put something away instead of putting it down. This is a favourite phrase of many decluttering gurus: '*Don't put it down, put it away.*'

Regardless of organizational style, the following three factors are essential for an organized and people-friendly home:

- Visibility
- Like with like
- Accessibility

To see or not to see . . .

Until recently, I wanted everything I used often, like skin-care products or cooking utensils, out on counters and visible. Once I moved into my small apartment, I realized that everything was getting very dusty, and it was driving me mad. Now I mostly store things neatly in drawers. Play around with what you want your rooms to look like. As long as all items have a home and are accessible, it's merely a choice of what looks and feels good to you.

There's a scene in the movie *It's Complicated* where Meryl Streep's character opens a drawer in her dressing table. All Nancy Meyer's movies look like they've been set-dressed from the pages of an interior magazine, but this scene stays in my mind for one reason. The drawer. Every single item had its own little compartment, even individual lipsticks. It is a thing of beauty. I dream of bespoke storage like this. Sadly, my life was not designed by Nancy Meyer's team and

I have to make do with the cut-and-paste DIY storage solutions I've developed over the years.

As I've mentioned, neat drawers are so important for keeping clutter at bay and for being able to find what we own when we need it. Beloved of Insta-organizers everywhere, storing items in a drawer standing up side by side rather than on top of each other will honestly change your life, like I mentioned before about tea towels in the section on kitchens in Chapter 5. Basically, nothing should be on top of something else in drawer storage. The aim is to get to a place where you can open a drawer or cupboard and see immediately what's in there. No pushing stuff around or pulling everything out to get what you need. If you can't see the second layer of items in a drawer or cupboard, then the storage is cluttered (gasp!) and needs reworking.

Like with like

Storing items of the same category together is essential to avoid duplicates. I can't tell you the number of clients who have three different bottles of cough syrup or Pritt Sticks or spatulas, when they really only need one at a time. The quantity is not the issue from this particular angle, it's the fact that we don't know what we have so we go out and buy another one, even though there were three of them hiding in our house! This is wasteful both of resources and time. Put a stop to it by keeping items like stationery, medications and DIY supplies all together. Then you can see exactly what you have and when it might run out.

Accessibility

You should be able to use your possessions without frustration. If every item has a place and that location does not change, it is easy to grab the item when needed and easy to rehome it after use. If housing, for example, your kitchen weighing scales in a box on a high shelf works for you, then that's fine. Others might need this item to be more reachable, not sealed up in a box but loose in a cupboard or on a kitchen counter. The aim with any system should be to make tidying things away as simple as possible. In a house where no items have specific homes, it is easy to get caught in a never-ending cycle of tidying. In a house where all items *do* have homes, even generally, tidying up is transformed from a daily struggle to a few simple actions that can be performed with very little thought.

Over-organized

For those of us who enjoy micro-organization with very specific categories, be warned against over-organizing too early in the process. When deciding where items should be stored post-declutter, start with larger categories, or your home will become a madhouse of piles! You can refine once your possessions have a general home. The most effective decluttering happens in stages, and the most effective organization does too.

Boxing

My long-suffering husband will tell you that I love boxes. Sometimes, he will come home and I will immediately drag him to see what I've done to organize the stationery drawer or the bathroom. I should be clear about what kind of boxes I advocate. I loathe old-fashioned jewellery boxes, as I think they are totally impractical, and I hate little trinket boxes, which tend to just gather dust. If used correctly, a few are fine, but I've seen many clients who are falling down with little weirdly shaped boxes which house never-worn jewellery and miscellaneous bits. Unless the box itself is of sentimental value, get it outta there. I remember holding on to a tiny matchbox-sized stack of decorative drawers which I'd had as a child. They were an absolute clutter trap, and when I realized that my emotional attachment to them no longer existed, out they went.

What boxes do I like? Any that you have already! You would be amazed what you actually have in your house that can help you get organized in a way that doesn't involve bringing in a load of ugly plastic containers.

1. Shoe boxes are the obvious first example, loved by both Marie Kondo and yours truly. I currently put my medicines and medications, my bicycle accessories and my winter gloves and hats in shoe boxes.

2. Boxes that once housed things such as greetings cards, candles, mugs, smartphones,

electrics – anything, really, that is sturdy and blocky. These can be useful to keep your spare coins in so they don't lie around the house, for example. I use a beautifully patterned box which contained a fancy mug to hold my make-up in a drawer. I also use a box which contained a toy dragon to keep my sewing equipment neatly organized, and an old chocolate tin to hold electrical wires. An old smartphone box has been the perfect home for Blu-Tack and Pritt Sticks.

3. Chocolate boxes – be creative! I've already suggested using a Ferrero Rocher box to store earrings. It genuinely works a treat, and looks great!

4. Tupperware that has lost its lid makes an amazing kitchen-drawer divider. I use one for items that might get lost in a larger kitchen drawer, like cocktail sticks and birthday candles. You could also use one to keep baking equipment such as cupcake holders and piping equipment.

Not only is this sustainable, it's extremely satisfying. If you find that you do need more boxes for storage, I would encourage you to seek out cardboard storage where possible. The world is quite literally drowning in plastic, and unless your items are being stored somewhere damp or really need to be visible from the outside, pick cardboard boxes.

Labels

Oh man, I love a label. As I have mentioned, you need to be able to see what you have in each cupboard and drawer without too much pushing and pulling. If you are putting a box of items somewhere hard to get at, like the top of a wardrobe, make sure to write a clear label stating what's in the box so that you can know at a glance instead of having to turn your room upside down looking for your summer clothes or the hats and gloves you packed away for when the weather gets cold again. Similarly, if a box with a lid is going in a drawer, label it so that, the minute the drawer is open, it's perfectly clear what's in there. It's impossible to keep mental tabs on every single item in our homes, and this system ensures that nothing gets lost. I would advise that you put labels on both the top and the sides of boxes so the contents can be stored at any angle.

Electrical items

I often wonder what my grandchildren (if I ever have any) will make of our fixation with wires and plugs. I imagine myself describing the desperate searches for a place to charge your phone and the anguish of leaving your laptop charger at home. We are a society awash with cables, and storing them can be a pain. After you have assessed which cables can stay and which should be recycled, my storage solution is a simple one: the humble rubber band. Wind a cable around your hand and use a rubber band to secure it at the midpoint. Be careful not to wind larger cables too tightly, as this can potentially damage them. Everyday items like phone chargers should be kept together, although most of us just leave them near a socket, which is grand. Lesser-used items like extension cables can be stored in a labelled box elsewhere. I'll give info on where to responsibly dispose of unwanted electronics in Chapter 13.

Paper

Paper organization is something that plagues many households, even though many of us now use paperless billing and online correspondence. When culling your collection of paper, be honest with yourself. Are you really going to use all those recipe cut-outs from magazines or are they just lying around making you feel bad for not being Nigella Lawson?

Any sentimental items that arrive in my house go into a discreet and easily accessible box that lives under my coffee table. When it gets full (which takes ages, as I'm quite practised in assessing what I'll actually want to keep), I go through it and put what's being kept in a large container I have in my wardrobe which houses all my memorabilia.

In terms of organizing, it depends on whether you are visually minded or prefer your paperwork out of sight. As I described already, some of us benefit from having the papers we need to act on visible, to jog our memories when they catch our eye. For someone with this disposition, I would advise investing in a noticeboard with categories. And if any papers need to be kept long-term, I prefer filing boxes, or a filing cabinet if you need more space. Accordion files that are hidden away in a drawer are inefficient and annoying, in my opinion. The same goes for a filing system that lives in an inaccessible place like the top of a wardrobe. Make life as easy as possible for yourself.

Research or seek professional advice about how long you are required to keep certain documents. I have had many clients who were terrified of throwing out paperwork but had no idea what they actually needed to retain. Doing this will save you lots of time and anxiety, as well as potentially freeing up space in your filing system.

If you use a filing cabinet, file categories in a straight line – put all the tabs in the same place along the tops of your folders. It's much easier on the eye and it's easier to add new folders to in the future.

I learned a great tip from the wonderful Maureen Gaffney's book *Flourishing*. Implement the OHIO rule for everyday post or other paper which may enter the house: Only Handle It Once. Basically, this means that once you open a piece of post and assess its contents, it is then stored in an appropriate place. For example, an outstanding bill would go on your noticeboard or wherever you keep your household 'to-do' list, items to be kept long-term should go to your filing system immediately, and unneeded papers can go straight to the recycling bin (remember that plastic windows on envelopes are soft plastic and therefore cannot be recycled). This is easy to agree with and difficult to implement into a busy, chaotic life – but give it a try.

Too much storage

I live in a tiny apartment with more or less zero storage space. Whatever I feel about wanting to value my possessions and be organized, my house is also clutter-free out of necessity. Our Christmas decorations and luggage live in our wardrobe and Danny's guitars decorate our living room. I have one large box of cards, letters, photos, diaries and memorabilia which also lives neatly in my wardrobe. However, most of my clients are middle-aged folk who have the luxury of owning their own home. A large house with lots of storage may seem like a dream living situation, but I've seen time and time again how too much storage provides a hidden home for broken or unwanted items. I've already mentioned the danger of avoiding making a decision about certain items and just putting them in the attic or the shed. Resist this temptation at all costs if you are lucky enough to have the extra space, and be ruthless in deciding what you actually want to keep. Just because you have the space doesn't mean you need to fill it all. An empty cupboard or shelf could be a wonderful rebellion!

Conclusion

Setting up the right systems for you and whoever you share your space with is so important if you want to stay organized and less cluttered for years to come. Getting to know what works for you can take time, but you will not regret it – this knowledge can be extremely liberating and reduce day-to-day stress. Above all, remember that it is not about how 'pretty' an organizing hack looks, but how easy it makes tidying things away every day for you. After this chapter of organizing advice, I am moving on to something which may seem completely contradictory, and may certainly seem sacrilegious to many of my fellow professional organizers – I want to talk about mess, chaos and disorder. And more importantly, why they are all perfectly normal parts of the human experience.

10

Leaving Space for Life

In defence of mess

And now for something completely different. I want to make the case for keeping things ... well ... a little bit messy. We have looked at the benefits of decluttering and organizing, but I often fear that only discussing tidiness is a one-dimensional approach to running our homes and lives. I think it is important to offer the other side of the coin, and this chapter looks at how we can allow space for the messiness of life, even from within a decluttered home.

One of the comments I hear frequently when someone learns what I do is: 'Your house must be so neat!'

In the interest of honesty, I want to come clean. Or, not so clean, as is often the case with my home. Let me take you on a virtual tour of the current state of my small apartment as it is on the day I write this. A pair of kicked-off shoes which belong in the bedroom lie under the coffee table, which is empty apart from two pig figurines and a candle. Last night's washing-up remains on the draining board. High Priestess of Lifestyle Optimization Gwyneth Paltrow has revealed that she 'can't sleep at night if there's dishes in the sink'. This is not something that has ever concerned me. A bag of electrical items gathered from clients sits in the hall waiting for me to drop them to the recycling centre. My floor could probably use a once-over with the vacuum cleaner. In my bedroom my small collection of shoes lies under the radiator, a few of them on their sides. A pile of clothes sits on the bed, waiting to be put back into the wardrobe.

I am not confessing to being a slob, I am confessing to being a normal person with a busy life. You might only learn that I'm into decluttering by looking at my storage. My drawers remain uncluttered, with their entire contents visible. Otherwise, my home looks pretty average; I would describe it as neat but lived in. You won't find it on any Instagram posts with the hashtag #minimalism attached. But Instagram was never designed to portray real life.

Creativity and mess

I had a client once who was an artist. She was adamant that we were never to touch her studio, which was a mess of paints, paper, objects, brushes and scraps of fabric. Without her clutter, she told me, her creativity would flounder. This instinct has been proven by several academic studies and anecdotal evidence from great thinkers who spare little thought for domestic neatness. Albert Einstein, the owner of a notoriously disordered desk, once posed the question, 'If a cluttered desk is a sign of a cluttered mind, of what, then, is an empty desk a sign?' Allowing mess some breathing room isn't just for artists and great thinkers. It is, frankly, inevitable in any full life. Anyone who loves baking, crafting or other hobbies that involve creating or collecting knows that mess is part of the process of enjoying these activities.

It is sometimes the case that mess and disorder can actually encourage creativity and new ideas. The most compelling book I encountered on this subject was *Messy: How to be Resilient and Creative in a Tidy-minded World* by Tim Harford. He passionately argues that 'real creativity, excitement and humanity lie in the messy parts of life, not the tidy ones', and loathes complex filing and organizing systems often imposed on workers by employers. If your chaotic and disorganized home feels cosy and normal to you, that's wonderful! It is only if disorder is causing a problem that it needs to be addressed. If the desire to have a pristine home is stopping you from pursuing activities that you might enjoy, like baking or doing art with your kids, I would encourage you to lean into a bit of mess and see where it leads you. Henry James wrote of one of his younger characters that 'the great shambles of life' was ahead of them. If I'm feeling that I'm not in control or that things are getting on top of me, I remind myself to relax into the great shambles of life! From there, things can be approached bird by bird. Let's have a look now at why we need this balance between mess and organization.

Order versus chaos

Psychologically speaking, all humans crave a balance of order and disorder, whether we are attempting creative endeavours or not. From an evolutionary point of view, order means repeated patterns which help us make accurate predictions such as what time of year to plant crops or when to hunt deer. The survival benefits are obvious. But elements of surprise, chance and novelty can also offer an advantage to humans. If we get too complacent with our routine, we can't react when things change, for example when a tiger suddenly appears on the road we walk every day without incident. We would never take risks and so never reap the benefits of an unexpected encounter or discovery. So it makes sense that we've developed a craving for both the predictable and the unpredictable. This fine balance is hard-wired into the oldest part of our brains. Art critics have observed that, although human beings have a deep psychological attraction to order, perfect order in art is uninteresting. This also applies to life, where predictability can become stifling.

As I explained in the introduction, my life has been a messy circus of career stops and starts, bouts of illness, wrong turns and huge waves of doubt. But it's all led me here, living a life of relative contentment, still struggling with my mental health from time to time but in a loving relationship and writing a dream-come-true book. The way I have gone about writing this book has been, true to form, anything but straightforward. I have worked on it between the not-insignificant events of my wedding and honey-moon, as well as other work, hen-party weekends, festivals and general life-living. I worked on the final edits whilst simultaneously writing a college dissertation on Sigmund Freud, all whilst in lockdown during the Covid-19 crisis. I initially worried that not having a proper writing routine would damage the quality of the book. Looking back, I now see that my ideas and writing are stronger from all the stops and starts. While I was away from my writing, ideas came to me that I know I would not have had by simply staring at my computer screen. I had conversations with people at social events I attended reluctantly which helped me join fiddly ideas together. As long as it's not stifling us, mess can open us up and fire off synapses which were long asleep. Embrace the chaos and the mess and the uncertainty – you might end up stumbling across what you've always wanted.

Ideal self versus chaotic reality

Allowing room for mess in our lives is vital if we want to free ourselves from the tight grip of perfectionism. Striving for *good enough* is a healthy and wise goal for any human, as we can see in the illuminating story of American poly-math Benjamin Franklin's failed efforts to lead a more organized life. At the tender age of twenty Franklin devised a list of thirteen rules for living a good life, based on his readings of ancient philosophy. The rules, which included temperance, cleanliness and humility, appeared in order of importance. Number three was order, and it advised to 'let all your things have their places; let each part of your business have its time'.

Franklin went on to have an extraordinarily productive professional life. He invented the lightning rod, which led to the development of electricity; he helped draft the American Declaration of Independence; he established the first American postal system ... I could genuinely go on for pages. Let's just say he was a high achiever. Yet he never quite mastered his goal of imposing order on his desk, home and affairs. In his diary, he confesses, 'my scheme of Order gives me the most trouble'. Tim Harford further explains that 'Franklin's diary and his home remained chaotic, resisting sixty years of focused effort from one of the most determined men who ever lived.' I love this. It's so real, so human, so gloriously imperfect. What's more, even at the end of his life, having admitted defeat in respect to order, Franklin has no regrets: 'But, on the whole, tho' I never arrived at the perfection I had been so ambitious of obtaining, but fell far short of it, yet I was, by the endeavor, a better and a happier man than I otherwise would have been if I had not attempted it.'

The ideal goal to aim for is the sweet spot between perseverance and self-acceptance.

Conclusion

I had a teenage client once whose bedroom floor was a clichéd mess of used towels, make-up and school books. When I was allowed to look in her wardrobe, however, I was amazed to find that everything was neatly folded and hung up, in stark contrast to the chaos outside. One size fits all doesn't work. The task is to find the balance that works for each of us and to relax into the inevitable messiness of life. One of my favourite pop-psychologists, Daniel Gilbert, has an excellent phrase in his book *Stumbling on Happiness* which I often think of: 'Human beings are works in progress that mistakenly think they're finished.'

It is foolish to claim that you can tidy your house once and never have to do so again. You will go through phases in life when you are very fit and phases when you are inactive, phases when your home is neat and phases when life takes over and it becomes messy again, phases when you're happy and phases that are hard. Tidying and organizing is not a video game that you reach the end of by defeating the final clutter monster. This is why I recommend leaving space for a little bit of mess as a reminder to go easy on yourself. 'Heresy!' I hear the decluttering Instagram stars say. But we all need a little mess somewhere to remind us that we're human and that no one, anywhere, is perfect. Breathe into the unpredictability of life and you might find yourself feeling, strangely, more in control than ever.

Part Five: Our Broken Relationship with Stuff

11

The Global System of Stuff

In this chapter I'll explore the global system of stuff. I'll use the fashion industry as a specific example of how, through what we own, we are connected to people and communities all over the world. Understanding where stuff comes from and appreciating the resources and human labour involved in its production has massively helped me change my habits. I hope this knowledge will do the same for you.

I do not believe owning and enjoying things is in some way *bad*. In fact, I believe objects are an essential and long-standing means of expressing identity and building community. It is easy to dismiss the desire for stuff as bad and unnatural, but that would be untrue and not very helpful. It is not the full story. Figures like St Francis of Assisi or the Buddha, who renounced all worldly goods in pursuit of spiritual enlightenment, are not humanity in its most natural form but exceptional outliers. There has never, ever existed a human society that has not adorned itself in some way or expressed itself through objects such as jewellery, fabrics, pottery, metalwork, and so on. This is the stuff of material culture and it is a core part of who we are. The idea of a lost human society from a simpler time untainted by materialistic tendencies is totally unhelpful. It makes us feel wrong and unnatural simply for following our instincts to create and express ourselves. The field of anthropology recognizes the practice of giving presents as an ancient human ritual. It has also been established that having more than what we need to survive, or being occasionally excessive, is bonding and joyful. Humans also instinctively crave experiences that are new and surprising; we want novelty as much as routine. As we know, however, the fast-paced modern world with its ever-changing array of cheap goods has wreaked havoc on our still-primitive desires and wants.

The global system of stuff

We need to get in touch with the actual physical reality of our things. We need to learn how to actually *see* them. The main problem I observe in my clients is that they are completely disconnected from the objects with which they share their lives. So few of us, when we buy something, stop to ask:

- Where has this come from?
- Who made this?
- Where will it go when I've finished with it?

I have a pepper mill at home which I bought in haste and without much thought. I recently looked at the label for the first time and saw that the pepper in it was grown in Vietnam but was packaged in South Africa. It now lives in a Dublin kitchen. *What?* I had to stop and reflect on how baffling and overwhelmingly strange this is. When we buy an item like this, we take part in a global system of production that is eye-wateringly complex. Did you know that the average T-shirt needs approximately eighty people (probably far more) to assemble it, if you take into account growing cotton, weaving, dyeing, printing labels, packaging and transporting? I can't begin to calculate the number of people who were involved in making my pepper mill. I think it's important to step back from what we buy and see the collaborative effort involved, even before you start to uncover the darker sides to how products are produced.

The people who profit from these systems of production make sure they are as invisible to the consumer as possible. Even when we do know, it's far too easy to look away. We know vaguely that sweatshops exist and that smartphones contain minerals that come from mines where human beings are enslaved, but we keep scrolling past these details or turn the page of the Sunday newspaper supplement. Most of us don't pay much attention. And I know, it can be overwhelming. When I first learned about this stuff, every purchase I made felt riddled with guilt. That stress quickly eased when I realized that it wasn't doing anyone any good. Guilt stifles action. These days, I feel empowered when I make informed decisions. I accept that I can't ever be 100 per cent ethical in my choices, because I live in a capitalist society. Messing up is unavoidable. But I also believe what Kim Stanley Robinson wrote in the *New Yorker* during the Covid-19 lockdown about how the production of our things is destroying our planet: 'this "knowing-but-not-acting" cannot continue'.

A brilliant art piece, *The Toaster Project*, by British designer Thomas Thwaite highlights the often absurd way modern objects are made. The project involved Thwaite building an entire toaster from scratch. And I mean *scratch*. He attempted to mine all the necessary minerals himself and smelt his own iron ore in a microwave. The outcome is a melted mess of wires and misshapen materials. It is funny, but it speaks so powerfully to what I'm trying to say. We need to start thinking about where things come from. From there, we are better placed to consume them in a more mindful and ethical way, to become more connected with our things and ultimately be more content with what we have.

The paradox of choice

Mass production of goods has brought prices down and increased consumer choice. This may sound like good news, but it has in fact led to consumers ending up far less satisfied with their choices. This phenomenon can be explained using psychologist Barry Schwartz's theory of the paradox of choice. His research looked at the vast amount of choice the modern consumer is presented with, from jams (both confectionary and musical) to cars to clothing. He found that the greater the number of options available, the less satisfying the final choice will be. I strongly relate to this. I find the carousel of movies on Netflix anxiety-inducing and I dread the daily discussion with Danny about what to have for dinner. (I once read that a relationship is one person asking the other what they want to eat until one of them dies. Nothing has ever seemed more profound.) Schwartz explains that 'as the number of choices grows further, the negatives escalate until we become overloaded. At this point, choice no longer liberates but debilitates.' I would highly recommend Schwartz's extremely popular TED talk on the subject. Marvel at the adorable nerdiness of his shorts and white sports socks and soak up the wisdom.

Too much choice leads to paralysis. And even when we do make a choice, we are less satisfied, which leads to self-blame as our minds seek a reason why we are unhappy. On a clutter level, if we are second-guessing our purchases as we make them, of course that will lead us to buy more and dispose of things freely. This is a bind that we must free ourselves from; if you learn to recognize when you're getting caught in these psychological traps, you can practise resisting them. Over time, trust me, the value that you place on what you consume will deepen, and so too will your contentment. Nowhere is the impact of too much cheap choice more visible than in the fashion industry.

My ethical awakening

I was twenty-three when I moved to London to study at the London College of Fashion, full of the blind optimism of youth. My plan was to build a career as a costume researcher for TV and film. Within two months, my dreams of corsets and top hats were forgotten; I had plunged head first into the world of anti-consumerism and sustainability and had joined the fight to save the Western world from its covetous and wasteful ways.

Everyone knew about sweatshops at this stage, and Naomi Klein's eye-opening book about corporate consumerism, *No Logo*, was everywhere. When I got to London I sought out events at which the humanitarian and environmental problems of the modern fashion industry were discussed. I was down the rabbit hole before I knew it, much to the dismay of my enthusiastic lecturers, who were trying to teach me that fashion was an undervalued form of art, to be revered and closely studied. They never once mentioned how the clothing we studied in such detail was produced. The dark underbelly of the fashion industry is shocking. Most of my fellow fashion students understood this but did not seem that bothered by it. They were happily researching fashion editorials and royal wedding dresses. I was campaigning at London Fashion Week wearing an organic cotton T-shirt with a dead fish on it. I'd gone deep.

My MA concerned the business model employed by most modern fashion retailers of cheap clothing that is made to be thrown away. This book is not the place to go into all the environmental and humanitarian problems of the industry, but I want to give you a short rundown of the most pressing issues. My aim here is to encourage you to stop and think before you buy your next item of clothing. It is vital that we all become more mindful of where and how our clothes are made.

The garment industry is often called capitalism's favourite child, and with good reason. Fashion is a business built around constant change and the constant need to buy things to keep up with the latest trends. Clothing has evolved from a product bought to last and be cared for into a disposable commodity that is often worn only a handful of times before it is dumped and another purchase is made. This affects our wallets, as I'll explain later on, but what effect has this explosion of choice had on our experience of buying clothes? Shopping for clothes has been sold to us as empowering and fun, and sometimes it is. More often than not, however, it can be a minefield littered with wrong decisions, shame and confusion. As we've learned through Schwartz's paradox of choice theory, the endless choices we are presented with can be massively stress-inducing. In order to shift more products, new designs come out in some shops *every day*. For someone who follows fashion diligently, this might be exciting, but for the majority of women this constant change in styles is confusing and often frustrating. Say you buy a jacket you love and wear it a few times, each time feeling good and happy with your purchase. Soon you realize that the jacket is now the 'wrong' colour or style; what you had previously thought was the height of fashion has now been replaced with something different. This causes dissatisfaction and more confused shopping.

Buying clothes that we wear a handful of times and then send to charity, at best, and landfill, at worst, is bad for our self-esteem. This is because making decisions about what to wear and how we want to present ourselves can cause anxiety at the best of times, but the fast-fashion model means that we have to make these decisions much more frequently than previous generations did. Even unconsciously, we can live in constant worry that our clothes are 'out of date'. Indeed, that is how the fashion industry *wants* us to feel, in order to get us back into the shops to buy more. As well as this pressure, cheap clothes can often fall apart after a few washes. This leads to a return to the shops and another potential dressing-room meltdown, or an impulse online purchase that turns out to be not what we wanted and then forget to return. It is no wonder that our wardrobes are fit to bursting.

All of this cheapness and disposability has brought huge profits to the industry and offers wide consumer choice, but it has had catastrophic effects on the environment, as well as creating inhumane working conditions for the people who make our clothes and, increasingly, those who sell them. The rise of online clothing giants like BooHoo and Pretty Little Thing has required large workforces to operate in gigantic warehouses (some in the UK), and during the Covid-19 crisis many workers complained of unsafe working conditions being maintained in order to satisfy customer demand. These retail giants have also been accused of incinerating returned orders rather than reselling them – that is how little these garments are worth. Across the fashion industry, the level of waste and disregard for human life is hard to comprehend. Below are quotes from two of my sustainable-fashion heroes.

'Fashion is fine as long as it doesn't harm anyone.
But fashion does harm people.'

– Kate Fletcher

'Fast fashion isn't free – somewhere someone is paying.'

– Lucy Siegle

Here's a tiny snapshot of the crisis:

- Large-scale clothing production is mostly unregulated in Asia and South America. Factories often rely on subcontractors in order to meet demands and these workers are not afforded the protections of international employment standards, often working forced overtime for nowhere near a living wage. When the Rana Plaza factory building in Bangladesh collapsed in 2013, 1,135 people were killed, despite workers' warnings about cracks in the walls. This is one of many such accidents which occur frequently in garment factories.
- The textile industry creates 1.2 billion tonnes of CO_2 a year, more than international aviation and shipping combined, consumes lake-sized volumes of water (approx. 2,700 gallons of water for one cotton T-shirt), and creates enormous amounts of chemical and plastic pollution (as much as 35 per cent of microplastics found in the ocean comes from synthetic clothing). Clothing made from synthetic, oil-based fibres such as nylon and rayon does not biodegrade and will sit in landfill releasing harmful fumes for hundreds of years.
- Textiles are the fastest-growing stream of household waste. Second-hand shops cannot cope

with the amount of low-value clothing being dumped on them and most of it is sent to markets in North Africa or burned. Thousands of bales of unsold products are simply incinerated at the end of the season by high-street brands.

- Where there were once two clothing seasons a year (summer and winter), there are now at least fifty-two, with many fast-fashion retailers both on- and off-line launching new products every single day. Significantly more trivial than the aspects listed above, the constant churn of style changes is arguably leading to a degradation of style and true fashion. I interviewed someone who worked for a fast-fashion brand as part of my research and they revealed how the pressure to keep up this pace has squeezed out the time and energy for creativity in this part of the industry: 'Most new collections are the same basic shapes but with different patterns. You get so sick of looking at the same stuff all the time.'

My hope is to leave you informed, but not hopeless; I believe that when we know more about the global fashion industry and understand the ways we can change our behaviour, it increases our satisfaction with our wardrobes. When you care about how things were made and where they came from, you learn to value them differently. This will not only prevent future wardrobe clutter but will help you get more joy from your clothes!

The un-humans of capitalism

I have a coat that I bought in Zara years ago (in the days of blissful ignorance) which I absolutely love and wear all the time. On the inside lining is a small gold label which reads 'handmade', as if to denote some kind of craftsmanship and elite value. This hugely irritates me. Here's the truth: *all* clothing is handmade. Touched by human hands. Human beings and human hands make our clothes.

In 2019 I attended a theatre performance which brought stories from the female garment factory workers of 1950s Dublin to life. It was an emotional experience for me. To see a line of women working at sewing machines and helping each other through the stresses of poverty and womanhood was so moving. As I left the performance space, I wondered how powerful it would be if we could imagine the daily lives of some of the women who make our clothes when we make fast-fashion purchases. Can we imagine them sharing news about their children or confiding in a friend about a health or financial problem? What I'm saying is, I wish we could see that the people who make our clothes are just that – people. These Asian and South American factory workers have been called the 'un-humans' of capitalism. We don't see them, so we pretend they do not exist. Our empathy cannot extend that far; in evolutionary terms, it was only designed to care for a couple of hundred people at most. How can it extend to people thousands of miles away we will never meet but whose hands have sewn our jeans? It's a question I'm still trying to answer. Will the recent establishment of garment factories in the UK by online retailers Pretty Little Thing and BooHoo make this problem feel closer to home? It is too soon to tell.

There was a time when the makers of clothing were seen as highly skilled workers. The International Tailors, Machinists and Pressers' Trade Union was founded in November 1908 by Jewish clothing workers hailing from the South Circular Road Dublin area where I currently live. I hope for a world where, when you buy a pair of jeans, you receive a card detailing who made them and what their circumstances are, whether they were paid fairly, and so on. If you'd like to learn more and help garment workers get a fairer deal from brands, you should follow the Clean Clothes Campaign.

Mindful clothing shopping

It is a simple truth that most of us own too many clothes. The speed at which clothing is produced and consumed cannot be sustained, given the Earth's finite resources. It's also important to note that higher prices do not always guarantee ethical practices. Many expensive brands use the same factories with the same standards as their cheaper high-street cousins. I do not want to leave you feeling despairing and apathetic. That would get us nowhere. I want to encourage readers to take a moment and *think* before they purchase something. Where did this come from? Who made it? Will I love it and look after it and will it add to my life? If we ask ourselves these questions, we might, over time, be able to slow down the endless churn of new garments and ease the pressure on garment workers. People ask me all the time where they should buy clothes. I am heartened that many ethical fashion brands now exist and can be found easily online. But I truly believe that *where* you shop is less important than *how* you shop. Boycotts of fashion brands have proven effective in the past, most notably against Nike in the 1990s, but they need to be organized en masse and there must be proper aftercare in place for any garment workers who lose their livelihood. Calls to boycott brands in recent years have rarely been accompanied by that same holistic process. The problem is hugely complex, and is frustratingly often reduced to pitting 'good' consumers against 'bad' consumers.

Sustainability and snobbery

There is sometimes an unfortunate tinge of judgement to anti-consumerism conversations, which does the movement no favours. Some of my favourite ethical-fashion commentators, such as Lucy Siegle and Aja Barber, feel that criticizing people for shopping in low-cost shops like Primark is motivated by a snobbery which detracts from the broader problems at hand. We don't talk enough about class in the sustainability realm. This is a nuanced issue too often seen in black-and-white terms. A concrete example of why it's faulty to view poorer shoppers as the root of the problem is that Primark and Selfridges are both controlled by the same billionaire family, Wittington Investments. You would never see an online outcry over a crowded Selfridges in the way you would with Primark. This played out in the media coverage of when shops re-opened after the lockdown lifted. The people queuing outside Brown Thomas were written about as patriotic contributors to the economic recovery. The people in Penney's were discussed in far less reverent terms. These culture wars get us nowhere.

We all need to understand that 'expensive' does *not* mean 'more ethical'. We all need to buy far less. We all need to demand higher-quality, longer-lasting products. We all need to demand that fewer goods are produced in the first place. We all need to actively push for a more equitable and safer world. We all need to educate those around us, but realize that they might not get onboard right away. We need to be sensitive to others' circumstances and experiences. Remember that you can't change how people behave or think by force. They have to get there by themselves. If you feel like that might take too long, and it probably will, use that frustration as an energizing force towards action, be it actively pressuring brands to do better, or campaigning for politicians who share your values.

Do what you can yourself, and don't judge anyone else.

Buy cheap, buy twice

One way to convert people to the need to buy less without mentioning sweatshops (which in my experience, sadly, often turns people off) is to point out that the financial logic of buying cheap becomes flawed when you realize that low-cost goods encourage excessive spending. This is an idea that most of us understand but which doesn't always filter through into behaviour change. As I continued my MA research, I asked many of my interviewees how they felt about saving up and buying fewer but higher-quality garments. Many of them said that this made sense on paper but was hard to put into practice. They described feeling bombarded by the availability of new items while at the same time feeling regret for the money they had already spent. One woman in her twenties told me, 'I've got so much crap and I've spent so much money. I think, "Oh my God, what is half this stuff? Where has my money gone? But then I go out and buy more, I can't resist."' Many of us are still caught in this cycle of mindless shopping. The desire for the new can be met in more sustainable ways, such as buying things second-hand, swapping items with friends and curating our possessions. These practices have become far more widespread in recent years, which is great cause for hope. The cheapness of products is, however, only one of the factors contributing to the mess we're in.

Disposability

Disposability is not a new idea. Toilet paper was common by 1900; paper cups and paper towels were adopted as sanitary measures in public places during the following decades, though few were yet used in homes. Disposable razor blades and bottle caps came into common use around the same time. People traditionally spent considerable time and effort

taking care of things: oiling and waxing, mending and altering, working to prolong the useful lives of the things they
owned. The transition to a throwaway consumer culture was
complex and gradual. The young and the wealthy embraced
new products first, while others lived as they always had. But
eventually the shift was complete, as people lost the knowledge of how to make things last, and the leftovers and scraps
they might once have repurposed or taken responsibility for
became rubbish.

By the middle of the twentieth century, more and more
products were manufactured and sold to be immediately
thrown away after one use. And people loved this new, con-
venient way of living, particularly women, whose domestic
work was decreased. As historian Susan Strasser wrote in
Waste and Want – A Social History of Trash, 'discarding things is
taken to be a kind of freedom'. Disposability rested on the
idea that somebody else would carry away the trash, that used
materials were worthless and that nobody need think about
what happened to them. The more we throw away, the more
we buy to replace what we've lost. Now major companies are
working hard to keep it that way.

Planned obsolescence and the right to repair

This morning, Danny asked if I'd seen his headphones. I
told him I hadn't but that he could borrow mine. 'Yours
don't fit my phone, though, my phone is an older model.'
The crafty folk at Apple had got us again. Planned, or built-
in, obsolescence is the economic concept of designing

products to break down or become outmoded quickly. How many kettles do you think you've gone through in your life? How many pairs of shoes? Products are not built to last, because that's bad for business. Manufacturers of daily items largely don't even bother to claim durability – that's how accustomed we, the consumer, are to things breaking down with no hope of fixing them. What's worse is that corporations are now coming after our desire to repair our broken items. Apple is among the worst companies for this, and there are several legal cases going on in the US over the so-called 'right to repair'. The members of this movement are campaigning for government legislation which would allow consumers to repair and modify their own electronic devices. This is necessary because often the manufacturers of such devices require customers to only use the services they offer; otherwise, the product's warranty is void. This policy ensures that fewer products are repaired, in order to encourage further purchases. It's a huge problem for farming equipment, too, and as a result has crippled many small American farmers, who can't repair their own tractors.

Many initiatives are cropping up across the globe to try and alter behaviours in favour of repairing and maintaining items long-term and ultimately help to stem the flow of disposable items. (I will provide information on specific resources in this area in Chapter 13.) The problem is that we've become so used to throwing something away when it's broken that this habit is hard to kick. Meanwhile, landfills bulge with busted toasters that could easily be fixed and, with each passing year, more repair skills are lost. Fortunately, in February 2020 the European Commission released its Circular Economy Action Plan, which seeks to compel manufacturers to design products that are sustainable, long-lasting and capable of being repurposed at the end of their lives. A key component of the plan is to establish a new 'right to repair' as part of EU consumer law, so that repair services, spare parts and repair manuals are available for all products. But ensuring that concrete initiatives are implemented to match these aspirations requires consumer pressure from us. There are, of course, certain products which many people are proud to have owned for upwards of forty years, such as the Kenwood mixer, which has remained unchanged in design since the 1960s. In praise of these durable bakers' friends, Libby Purves wrote in *The Times* that 'these hulking creatures are a standing reproof to our age of built-in obsolescence.' My mother still proudly uses a plate warmer once owned by her parents, and a close friend trots out the same Christmas lights she inherited from her father year after year. This pride in owning things that last already exists, we simply need to demand that it can be extended to all our possessions.

Throwaway society – where does our rubbish end up?

'Waste is the negligence of privilege.' Out of context, this sentence could be read as the utterings of some sort of malicious recycling robot bent on destroying all those who mindlessly dispose of precious resources. I found it in *The Craftsman*, a book by American sociologist Richard Sennett that encourages us to appreciate craftsmanship in all its forms, from a cleverly designed vacuum cleaner to a well-written piece of computer code. Something those of us who live in wealthy countries don't stop to think about much is where things go after we are finished with them. A bin is only a recent human innovation. Many indigenous communities around the world still do not understand the concept of a bin or throwing something away. Let's break down that phrase, 'throw away'. Where is this magical land of *away* where our rubbish goes? Think about it. We operate on an out-of-sight, out-of-mind policy in regard to how our possessions are made and how they are disposed of. We don't think about heaving landfills or incinerators, but we are directly connected to them every day. It is essential that we reconnect with every stage of an item's life if we are to truly value our possessions and consume more sustainably.

Plastic not so fantastic

The rise of plastics as the material of choice for the current age has warped our sense of connection to how things are made. Plastic requires consumers to buy things rather than make them, to throw things out rather than fix them. Nobody makes plastic at home, hardly anybody understands how it is made and it usually cannot be repaired. It also cannot return to nature by biodegrading. None of this has stopped the ever-increasing production of plastic. In fact, nearly half the plastic ever produced has been manufactured since 2000. Nearly half. And most of it still exists somewhere in the world, at best as a recycled eco-shirt or bottle, at worst languishing in a dump in Southeast Asia. I'll let you in on a dirty little secret: recycling plastic is largely a scam. The practice of individual recycling was in fact developed and promoted by the plastic and oil industries themselves as a way to place the responsibility for waste with the consumer, whilst allowing plastic production to increase unquestioned. Recycling plastic is considerably more complex and technical than turning rags into paper or melting down metals. A plastic bottle can only be recycled once, unlike glass or metal, so to treat these materials as equally renewable is wildly inaccurate. Even so-called 'compostable' plastic products require very specific conditions in order to break down fully. They should not be treated as a long-term solution but are mostly examples of 'greenwashing', which means companies jumping on the eco-bandwagon with the least expense possible. In Ireland, our recycling facilities are very limited and most waste is shipped overseas to be processed. It's also clear that many households are confused about, and perhaps disrespectful of, their recycling bin. Speaking to the *Irish Examiner* in 2018, Irish Packaging Recycling managing director Des Crinion said that his facility is constantly awash with unrecyclable materials such as nappies, aerosol cans and old shoes, which makes efficient recycling near to impossible. Our recycling behaviours and attitudes have to change. We need clearer guidelines from our governments, but we also need to take responsibility and seek out the correct information ourselves from www.mywaste.ie in Ireland and www.wrap.org.uk in the UK. I think it's just as important to know what can't be recycled as to know what can. If more of us understood the limits of the process, there could be far less contamination of the recycling centres and more valuable resources could be saved from landfill.

The invention of plastic has led to incredible innovations in science and technology and should not be demonized across the board. People's lives are saved daily by medical procedures which were not possible without plastic. But with much plastic comes much responsibility. We need to vastly reduce how much single-use plastic is produced in the first place. The intense focus on personal recycling is a smokescreen for the lack of corporate action on climate change. It places the onus for change too heavily on the consumer. The belief that the enormous existential problems of climate emergency and environmental destruction can be fixed if all of us just get better at recycling is not only dishonest but dangerous. Yet we continue to separate our rubbish and consume as we always have with impunity, while the large corporations who contribute the most to carbon emissions operate business-as-usual. It is victim-blaming madness. And that blame paves the road to apathy, which can really seal our doom. But this doesn't mean we should do nothing. We need to step away from our reliance on recycling towards the better practice of refusing as much packaging as we can. My friend Pat Kane runs Reuzi, a Dublin-based minimal-waste shop. She reworked a classic line from the film *Notting Hill* that has stuck in my mind, and I hope will stick in yours too: 'I'm just a girl, standing in front of a recycling bin, asking you to avoid it.'

Conclusion

Understanding the life cycle of our stuff, from its produc-tion to its disposal, can help teach us how to place a higher value on what we buy and own. The aim is to gain a deeper appreciation of the work that goes into all items, from clothing to kitchenware. We cannot buy our way out of this mess; we should use our energy to elect politicians who share our values, and keep the pressure on brands to adopt better practices across the board. Getting in touch with the reality of how inadequate our waste and recycling systems are can also motivate us to reduce the amount of stuff we send to any bin (recycling or landfill). Once you see behind the curtain of the global production system, it is hard to look away, but it leads to a deeper connection with your possessions and can help wean you off clutter for good.

12

How to Love Our Stuff Again

We've learned that by decluttering and organizing our homes we can discover the objects that truly matter to us. But how can we retrain ourselves to truly love the things we already own and place a higher value on future purchases? This will not only lead to deeper personal satisfaction, but could help contribute to a change in how products are produced globally. We, the consumers, have lots of power if we act en masse. If I didn't believe that, I would never have written this book.

It's also important to point out at this stage that having enough stuff to be able to get rid of some of it is a freedom only open to a small percentage of the world's population. To put it plainly, participating in the decluttering craze is a privilege. Most people have to make do with what they have, regardless of the measure of joy they get from their things. Several thought pieces have argued that to live as the decluttering darlings advocate requires a faith in a continuing abundance and prosperity that many people were not raised to expect. For these families, to dispose of belongings that are 'perfectly good' simply because they don't make you *feel* a certain way is a heresy. This is a belief system handed down by frugal parents who teach that objects have value because you bought them with your hard-earned money or acquired them through fate or some stroke of savvy, and if they're not totally broken or torn, their value is everlasting. Many people simply can't afford to do with less and have a more complex relationship with their things beyond a yes/no answer about joy. The fear of scarcity is very real for millions of people. For those of us who have the privilege of not thinking too hard about our possessions, it would do us no harm to reflect on these families and communities who never took what they had for granted.

Objects of affection

How can we fall back in love with our possessions? As part of my research for this book, I met with Brenda Malone, who is the Curator of Military History at Ireland's National Museum. I already knew Brenda through a theatre company I once worked for and I knew she was passionate about objects and their stories. The main theme that emerged from our chat was: *How do you teach people to value things?*

This is the key issue we need to tackle in order to improve our relationship with our stuff on both a personal and a global level.

Brenda wonders how the items she shares her life with will be treated when she dies. How will her executors know the story behind a vintage wine decanter or a seemingly valueless travel souvenir? This reminded me of the potter Edmund de Waal's bestselling memoir *The Hare with Amber Eyes*, in which he attempted to trace the story behind a collection of Japanese *netsuke* (miniature sculptures) which he had inherited. By unearthing their history, de Waal grew more attached to the objects and their value for him increased. Our great poet Seamus Heaney wrote a beautiful piece of prose where he details the delight to be found in old objects:

> When we gaze at an ancient cooking pot or gaming board or the shoe of a Viking child or a medieval child's drawing, we are exercising a fundamental and primary part of our nature.

That primary part of our nature is our capacity to connect with objects and to see them as a meaningful part of the story of our lives. When we connect in this way, the value an object holds increases tenfold. Heaney also described the forgetten objects he found at the top of an old wardrobe as 'dormant energies' which held 'meanings that could not be quite deciphered'. A regular Marie Kondo. Speaking of Kondo, I feel it would be useful to take a closer look at her ideas. Sadly, most of the wisdom and nuance of what she is saying has been lost on Western commentators. And she lost some of her credibility with me when she launched her own product line, which included essential items such as a $75 'self-care' tuning fork (Gwyneth Paltrow must be involved somehow). But, as you'll see, I believe that the core of her philosophy has huge value.

Shintō

Japanese culture has for centuries been steeped in reverence for the material world. Marie Kondo explains that Japanese people have an 'ingenuity born out of the constraints of living in small spaces in Japan' and that 'a love for orderliness [is a] national trait'. The Shintō origins of Kondo's philosophy are often brushed over, but I found an illuminating explanation of them by the author Margaret Dilloway, whose mother was a Japanese practitioner of the Shintō religion. As a child, Dilloway was instructed by her mother to 'clap three times so the *kami* know you're here'. Kami are Shintō spirits present everywhere – in humans, in nature, even in inanimate objects. Dilloway explains, 'At an early age, I understood this to mean that all creations were miracles of a sort. I could consider a spatula used to cook my eggs with the wonder and mindful appreciation you'd afford a sculpture; someone had to invent it, many human hands and earthly resources helped get it to me, and now I use it every day.'

This is the very root of what I want to communicate with this book: that objects come from somewhere, are made by someone and should be cherished accordingly. Once we begin to change how we view our things, our problems with overbuying, dissatisfaction with what we have, and clutter itself may fall away. If they happen on a large scale, changes like these will undoubtedly have a positive impact on our environmental crisis.

Kondo certainly wants us to treat objects with due respect.

Her philosophy is almost shamanic in its desire to view objects as if they had real feelings. Take for example her famous/infamous reverence for socks, which, in her words, 'take a brutal beating in their daily work, trapped between your foot and your shoe, enduring pressure and friction to protect your precious feet . . . The time they spend in your drawer is their only chance to rest.' What we in Europe and America read as adorable eccentricity is actually, for Kondo, a spiritual practice.

By describing her appearance as cartoon-like, doll-like or othering her because of her 'adorable' lack of English, many commentators are perpetuating the long history of colonial countries fetishizing Asian women, and they miss the valuable insights she has to share. I guess if I'm being fully honest, I'm fetishizing and appropriating Japanese culture by admiring their attitude to objects without fully understanding the Shintō religion. Uncomfortable to admit, but true nonetheless. However, if we can peel back the racism, what the global response to Kondo reveals is just how disconnected we are from our possessions. Seeing her Netflix clients glance at each other warily as Kondo meditatively greets their home makes me think we all need a solid dose of Shintō in our lives.

Wonder

We all naturally give some of our belongings more meaning than others without even thinking about it. If we can take notice of these meaningful items and why they matter, that level of care can ripple out to other over-looked items.

Danny and I have lots of small household items that we both really care about, like the beautiful wooden candlesticks made by our friend, or a framed print of a Seamus Heaney poem which we received as a wedding gift. Where these things came from and what we associate them with matters. The thing I have the most of, by far, are books. They are everywhere, and I highly value each one of them. When I emerged from my worst bouts of depression, I read my Harry Potter books, which I've had since I was a child. They required no effort or concentration to read but allowed me to escape in a way that TV couldn't quite manage. Recently, Danny started reading Harry Potter, having never tried the books before. He turned to me in bed mid-read the other night and said, 'It's extra special to me that these are *your* Harry Potter books I'm reading.' These books have become part of our story, and storytelling matters; it is one of the best techniques to practise to help rewire our relationship with our stuff.

Humans are not only *homo sapiens*, we are *homo narrans* – storytellers. If stories help us make sense of our lives and bind us to the objects in our homes, can we create stories for everything we own? A romantic idea, yes, but I think it might work. Let me try this thought experiment out on myself right now. I have never given the keyboard on which I type much notice, but now I am looking at it properly for the first time. It is wireless, so I can have my laptop screen at a height that is safe for my neck. Danny bought it for me for this purpose, so a big part of this object's story is love and care. I look at the white keys and the silver board and wonder where these materials came from, and who made and assembled them, how many people were involved, how many countries, how much time and expertise went into making it. We take this stuff completely for granted, but we must remind ourselves how lucky we are to own such items. This keyboard is so useful to me, and I have achieved so much with its help. Now, you might call me a crazed hippie – and you wouldn't be the first. I have a vivid memory from years ago when I lived in a houseshare with several friends. I had decided, characteristically on a whim, to cook red cabbage. When I sliced open the purple dome I was struck by the beauty of the swirls I found inside. To me, it was art. I rushed excitedly into the living room to show my housemates, but they were predictably mocking. 'Classic Emma', one said, fondly (I think). 'Lost in her hippie mind.' I'll hold my hands up and say that mine was perhaps not a typical response to an everyday vegetable, but I would argue that the reaction brought me joy and should not be dismissed.

A phrase I have loved since I was in my teens comes from the inspirational Irish social entrepreneur, writer and Catholic nun Sister Stanislaus Kennedy, or Sister Stan, as she is known. She writes that 'to take for granted is the death of wonder'. Read the sentence back slowly again. So much wisdom in only a few words. Sister Stan's philosophy echoes the Japanese philosopher and folk-craft advocate Soetsu Yanagi, who writes, 'When one becomes too familiar with a sight, one loses the ability to truly see it.'

Soetsu Yanagi's essay collection *The Beauty of Everyday*

Things (written between 1933 and 1947) was published in English in 2019. The book is a celebration of *zakki*, or 'miscellaneous things' – ordinary kitchen utensils, handy tools and implements not meant for display or decoration but for everyday use. He observes that it is easy to love our treasured possessions, but what about the items we use every day with little thought?

When I refer to the beauty of ordinary objects (*zakki*, or 'miscellaneous things'), you may think I am being intentionally eccentric or perverse. In order to forestall erroneous views and associations like this, I will here list a few cautionary notes. *Zakki* basically refers to the various utensils and tools made use of by the great mass of common people. As such, they could be called *mingu*, 'people's implements'. They are ordinary things that anyone can buy, that everyone comes regularly into contact with in their daily lives. They cost very little and can be procured almost anywhere and at any time. They are familiarly referred to as *temawari no mono* ('the handy'), *fudan-zukai* ('the ordinary'), or *katte-dogu* ('kitchen implements'). They are not meant for display or decoration; they are seen in the kitchen or scattered here and there throughout the house. They are plates; they are trays; they are chests; they are clothing. Largely, they are things for family use. All of them are necessary for everyday living. There is nothing unusual or rarefied about them. They are things that people are thoroughly familiar with, that they know through and through. However, there is one thing that never ceases to amaze me. Though these objects are the most familiar to us throughout our lives, their existence has been ignored in the flow of time, because they are considered low and common. It is as though these beautiful objects had no redeeming features.

Soetsu goes on to say that 'we no longer look upon objects as we used to, which is undoubtedly due to their poor quality.' This is definitely a large contributing factor to our dismissive attitude to everyday items. We have already covered how the drop in price and quality as a result of mass production has impacted our attitudes to clothes, but this is applicable to everything we own. I am passionate about encouraging all of us to value *everything* we own, even the cheapest and lowest-quality items. It is easy to want to take great care of a designer handbag or an expensive wine glass, but the change of attitude that I want to see is all of us treating everything we own equally, from our cheapest T-shirt to our most glamorous dress. Every item has a use, an aesthetic value, or both. This leads me on to the most often quoted decluttering mantra: *Have nothing in your house that you do not know to be useful, or believe to be beautiful.*

It really is as simple as that. If we view something as truly useful, we will be more inclined to repair and maintain it, and if we believe something to be beautiful, it will always have value. The writer of this much-loved phrase was the British artist William Morris, who was a key figure in the Arts and Crafts movement of Victorian England. Think of Liberty in London, with its famous floral prints – Morris was one of their original designers. The movement saw artists and thinkers campaigning for a return to pre-industrial craftsmanship and a slowing down of material production. I imagine Soetsu and Morris might have got on very well if they'd ever met.

Conclusion

Streamlining our possessions is one thing. The heart of the matter lies in how we relate to the objects in our lives. For me, this is the most important chapter of the book. I hope it has left you with a renewed sense of wonder and a greater appreciation for the complexity of the world of things. During the Covid-19 lockdown I observed many people around me slowing down enough to feel grateful for all sorts of things. I hope these practices of slow gratitude can continue in the years to come.

Part Six: Changing Your Ways for Good

13

Sustainable Change

It's a difficult process to declutter a life and a home. That's why it's important to make sure the clutter doesn't build up again in the future. We've already learned the many reasons why our houses came to be filled with stuff we don't need in the first place. Now let's explore strategies for turning this new knowledge into sustainable change.

Mindful shopping

There's a story that is told again and again within my circle of girlfriends from college. Two of them attended a weight-loss motivation group (neither of them needed to change in any way, and still don't, by the way), and the woman who ran the group turned out to be quite the character. Whilst pontificating on the evils of certain foods, she posed a question to the group which immediately gained cult status when it was relayed to the rest of us afterwards. She asked:

When is a good deal not a good deal *for you*? You know when you're out shopping and you see five chocolate bars for a euro? You think, 'Great, I'll pick them up for the kids,' and into the basket they go. What you *should* ask yourself is whether or not this is a good deal *for you*, otherwise where will those bars end up?

The answer came in a chorus from the regulars of the group, as if they were worshippers in church declaring the word of the Lord: '*In your mouth!*'

Now, this story is problematic in terms of shaming women for eating and penalizing certain foods as 'bad'. But we can reframe it to help you be more mindful when you're out shopping.

Scenario: While out shopping or while browsing innocently online, you come across an item you never thought you'd need or want. Somehow, you feel compelled to buy it because it's 'a bargain'. Stop, think of my story, and ask yourself:

Is this a good deal *for me*?
Where will this item end up?
Answer: *In my house!*

It's so easy to allow clutter into our homes these days because stuff is So Bloody Cheap, and online shopping means we can invite new clutter into our homes from the comfort of our couch without much thought. Always remember the endowment effect, and how much easier it is to buy something than to get rid of it. Slow and mindful shopping really is a key habit to adopt to prevent clutter from building up.

Another potential pitfall is to see a decluttering session as an excuse to go out shopping to refill your thinned-out wardrobes and empty shelves. A friend of mine conducted research on the relationship between young female consumers and their clothing-disposal habits and found that bringing a bag of clothes to charity can provoke a feeling of well-being often followed by a shopping trip because 'they deserve it'. *Beware* this psychological trap. Remember how much you wanted your wardrobe to be cleared out in the first place. Resist the urge to splurge, and bask in the glory of an empty shelf!

Habits

It's all very well to advise adopting better habits but, as I know all too well, it can be hard to make them stick. I've bitten my nails for as long as I can remember. I've genuinely tried everything to kick this habit, but my nails remain stubby moons on the tops of my fingers, and I am gently mocked by relatives who can't believe I still do it. I currently have two large Post-its stuck on the wall above my desk: one says, 'DRINK WATER!!'; the other says 'STRETCH!!' They are the latest in a long line of techniques that I've tried in an attempt to develop new habits.

I know how hard it is to break a well-worn way of doing something, even if it is no longer working. Personal change is hard-won and happens in cycles; we come back to the same hurdles again and again, and that's okay. Each time, hopefully, we've learned one more small thing that'll make jumping that hurdle a little easier. If you're struggling to develop good habits as regards organizing your home or shopping mindfully, it's okay. As I've said numerous times in this book, life is messy and frayed at the edges. I know it's a cliché, but there's so much wisdom in Samuel Beckett's oft-quoted line: 'Ever tried. Ever failed. No matter. Try again. Fail again. Fail better.'

I fail better every day and I've learned to not let it dictate my self-worth. At times when my mood is low, old bad habits will re-emerge like evil spirits lying in wait to catch me off guard. Lasting change has to take root in our brain stem, and the ground there is hostile to outsiders. Old habits die hard. New ones take time to form. If you're really struggling, operate on an *anything counts* policy – if you do fifteen minutes of a task instead of the one hour you'd hoped for, it still counts.

Apart from adapting to the tweaked flow of your home, another habit I would suggest cultivating is a clutter check-in maybe once a month. It can just be an hour, but take time to survey your house and discover if clutter is creeping back in anywhere. Schedule this time in your diary and show up to it, as you would an exercise class. This simple practice will help you become more alert to clutter and can prevent you becoming overwhelmed in the future.

Sustainability and mindful disposal

I love helping people declutter and streamline their lives. I get the same kick out of making sure as little of their unwanted stuff as possible becomes rubbish. Although this can seem daunting after a large declutter, I hope that this extra layer of work on my part plants the seeds of better disposing habits. In my most idealistic daydreams, I imagine a world that emulates Eskilstuna in Sweden, where no domestic waste goes to landfill. Residents of the former steel-industry town, 'the Sheffield of Sweden', sort their waste into seven multicoloured categories at home (green for food, pink for textiles, grey for metal, yellow for paper, blue for newspaper, orange for plastic and black for mixed) and, for the past four years, people have been able to drop off their unwanted goods for recycling at ReTuna, the world's largest second-hand mall. Yes, not just one shop, a whole shopping centre! ReTuna's founder and manager Anna Bergström explained in an interview with the *Guardian*:

> When I first came here, no one knew about the mall. And when they did, no one liked it. In a town like this, which has suffered, people are suspicious of change, especially something as radical as a shopping mall where all the goods are donated by the people of the town and then resold to them.

Now ReTuna is full of shoppers roaming around second-hand stores, looking at everything from furniture to children's toys, flowers and clothes. The mall is situated in an unassuming warehouse building in the middle of a field, next to one of the town's two recycling centres. 'Everyone's minds began to change the day we opened,' says Bergström. 'Six thousand people came to visit that day, and since then we average 700 visitors a day and 300 tour groups a year.'

Without a nearby ReTuna, how can we start disposing of our unwanted items responsibly?

Many clutter items like good-quality clothes, books and paper have obvious destinations outside our home (charity shops and recycling bins). What's not so obvious is deciding what to do with items such as unused shoe bags, shampoo samples, half-used make-up, and so on. Here's a list of tips on how to deal with a selection of things that can cause panicked households to chuck them in a nearby skip. There are always better options, I assure you.

- Periodicals such as *National Geographic* can sometimes be donated to schools or nursing homes – double-check with your closest school and local homes. (Most charity shops no longer take them, sadly.) If they cover a specific area, try and contact a group that might be interested. For example, I had a client recently who gave her old art textbooks to an art college library, and another who donated a collection of crafting magazines to the Design and Craft Council of Ireland.

- Unopened cosmetics and personal-hygiene items are accepted by a number of women's shelters. Call before you donate. If you have half-used make-up, maybe host a swapping party with friends who might love that shampoo that you didn't like the smell of. Involve clothes in the swap, too, and that's a party!

- Beauty samples and hotel toiletries. Use them or lose them. I have a friend who has a huge collection of these that she intends to use for travelling, but she can never find the samples when she's packing. My advice is to keep them in a labelled box somewhere you will remember when travelling, maybe even inside your empty suitcase. If you still fail to use them, take them to a women's shelter and swear never to let them enter your wash-bag again.
- DVDs/CDs/even VHSs. Many people still use these and do not consider them clutter. Coming from a family of art-house-cinema lovers, I am aware that certain films and series are only available on DVD and would be difficult to source online. What I find odd are the people who only use their TVs for streaming services but still remain wedded to their DVD collection. I think this is perhaps back to the money-guilt idea; these items were paid for and are therefore valuable, even if they are useless. One way to get around this guilt might be to find a friend who still uses DVDs and gift them a selection of yours which you know they'll watch. As ever, be considerate to your friend and avoid clutter-dumping! You could also make a list of your collection to store the memory of your evolving tastes. If you want to keep DVDs for sentimental reasons, that is of course totally legitimate. Do try to be honest with yourself, though, and if the root

cause of your reluctance turns out to be financial,
do your best to work through the sunk cost and
let go.

Most European countries have a long way to go before
any of our towns reach the heights of innovation and effi-
ciency of ReTuna but, thankfully, we have many initiatives
which can help declutterers who want to take responsibility
for their waste. Websites such as eBay and donedeal.ie/
donedeal.co.uk are the obvious suggestions for re-selling
items, but I would also recommend Freecycle, operating
in both the UK and Ireland, which allows users to post
items they no longer need and give them away for free. It's
similar to the American practice of leaving unwanted but
still useable furniture on the street to be picked up by
whoever gets there first. There's a great website called
www.repairmystuff.ie which links people to skilled workers who can repair anything from clothing to lawnmowers.
The Restart Project in the UK offers a similar service.

Many charities accept furniture, my favourite in Dublin
being Age Action. If you want some amazing furniture, visit
their warehouse – the gems you find there you wouldn't
believe. As I mentioned already, dropping off a bag to charity can leave us with a sense of well-being, as if we have
contributed to the greater good. Of course, it is better to
send things to charity than to landfill, but I would gently
advice against using charities as a general dumping ground
to relieve us of the guilt of our waste. It is far more sustainable, and ultimately more satisfying, to seek out a direct
home for our unwanted goods so that we know they will be

used. Charity shops are great for clothes, shoes and small household items, but what about toys, baby equipment and electrics, and so on?

Below are some of my favourite companies who can take pre-loved items and use them for good.

- The Rediscovery Centre makes upcycled clothing and furniture out of donated goods, based in Ballymun, Dublin: www.rediscoverycentre.ie
- Camara recycles old computers for use in low-income schools, mainly in Africa: www.camara.org
- Recycle It is a wonderful non-profit initiative based in Ballymount, Dublin, which recycles all sorts of items, including electronics and furniture: www.recycleit.ie
- Smalls for All is a charity which sends gently used bras and underwear to women in need in both the UK and certain African countries: www.smallsforall.org
- Swedish Stockings recycles worn-out or torn tights: www.swedishstockings.com
- Thriftify is basically an online charity shop, a platform that automatically values and sells items online, connecting consumers with charities across the UK and Ireland: www.thriftify.ie
- Terracycle is a wonderful company which recycles traditionally non-recyclable items like crisp packets and personal-care product bottles: www.terracycle.com

- Runner's Need is a UK-based running-supplies company which accepts old, worn-out runners: www.runnersneed.com/about-us/recyclemyrun
- Certain women's shelters will accept baby and children's items, but always contact your local shelter to make sure before making a donation. Children's charities such as Barnardo's sometimes accept toys and children's books.
- Worn-out towels and sheets can be donated to animal shelters, where they are used for bedding. In Ireland, Liberty's recycling banks shred surplus cotton material into cleaning wipes for local customers, including Dublin Bus, motor factories and cleaning companies. Their clothing banks are available across the country: www.libertyrecycling.ie. Several similar services operate in the UK including: www.uktextilerecycling.co.uk

I had a gorgeous experience with the Freecycle Network when I was keen to rehome a barely used exercise cushion and a set of paper filing boxes. I could easily have dumped them on my local charity shop and expected them to deal with the problem. Out of sight, out of mind. Instead I posted the items on Freecycle and, within a few hours, I met a woman who worked in an underfunded school and who was thrilled to receive these items. She intended to use the cushion as a sensory tool for one of her autistic students. I felt so good knowing that my unwanted stuff was going somewhere where it would be used, and it proved that we often can't imagine how useful some of our unwanted stuff can be to other people in our community.

A note on zero-waste lifestyles

Some sustainability advocates live extreme zero-waste life-styles where they aim to throw away as little as possible and try to fit their year's landfill waste into a single jam jar. We see them proudly displaying their achievements online, making it look easy and fun to live this way. These activists have value in that they provoke discussions and can prompt those of us outside their lifestyle to question our own habits, but I do worry that these influencers could be veering into the same perfectionist and self-optimizing realm that we see in wellness culture. In reality, you need to be rich both in money and, crucially, time if you want to be a perfect zero-waster. I suppose it's useful to have a standard to aspire to, but I have been to certain zero-waste events at which people can be judgemental if someone whips out a disposable baby wipe or forgot to bring their keepcup. Life is never perfect, and neither is trying to live more ethically. I fear that this behaviour may turn people off and have in fact heard friends express the concern that if they can't get it all right, then what's the point. An essential sustainability rule to live by is one often seen on social media: we do not need a small number of people 'doing' sustainability perfectly, we need masses of people doing it imperfectly. *Minimal* waste is a far more realistic goal to set yourself if you are thinking of embarking on overhauling your home and lifestyle. Swimming against the tide of convenience can be hard at times, but the more each of us does, the greater our collective impact will be. Go easy on yourself and remember that perfect is always the enemy of better.

Changing how we view property

Comedian Steven Wright has a joke that's more like a Zen mantra: 'I have the world's largest collection of seashells. I keep it on all the beaches of the world . . . perhaps you've seen it.'

A big switch that many of us need to make is that you don't have to own something for it to have value to you. Why does a whole estate of houses need individual ladders in each house? Why do we all need our own rooftop box for the car? Could you see a time when it might be normal to rent such items for when they are needed? If this triggers your fear of scarcity, take a minute to think about how frequently you use items like those I've just suggested. Wouldn't it be cheaper to rent or borrow them when you needed them? And wouldn't it build a sense of community that we are sorely lacking? There is an initiative called the Library of Things which has taken place in several cities, including Dublin. The project involves offering seldom-used items like tools and garden equipment for rent to members of the public. If this initiative was rolled out more widely, it could lead to a healthy shift in our attitude towards our stuff.

The rental of clothing is rapidly expanding within the

fashion industry, particularly for event and maternity wear. Clothing-swapping events are becoming more popular too, but a word of caution if you've never been to one before. When items are offered for free, they can take on a strange force whereby we cannot assess their use apart from the fact that they cost nothing. I came away from my very first clothes swap, way back in London in 2011, with a pair of pink knee-high boxing boots and a dress that was too small for me. Now I see the prospect of accepting free second-hand goods as an exercise of restraint and common sense. As with anything I buy, I do my best to come home from a swap with only items that I really love.

Conclusion

We know how perfectionism can trip us up and why that happens. I want to emphasize again the importance of aiming for 'good enough', and building from there. If you are making an effort to be more mindful in your shopping and disposal habits, but you see your friend is doing more, don't let that stop you from doing what you can. Shaming yourself or anyone else gets us nowhere. As I've said, change happens in small waves, not tsunamis. At the risk of having to rename this book *Ways to Appropriate Japanese Culture*, I suggest you take inspiration from *wabi sabi*, the Japanese art of appreciating the beauty in the naturally imperfect world. *Wabi sabi* is an ancient aesthetic philosophy rooted in Zen Buddhism. It concerns a traditional reverence for prized bowls that were handmade and irregularly shaped, with uneven glaze and cracks. These seemingly damaged objects, viewed through the lens of *wabi sabi*, possess a perverse beauty in their deliberate imperfection. Accepting the world as imperfect, unfinished and transient, and then celebrating that reality, can be incredibly freeing. Perfectionism can paralyse us. I used to think that if I wasn't up and at my desk by a certain time, the whole day was a write-off, or if I only jogged for twenty minutes instead of forty-five, that twenty minutes didn't count at all. I had outright failed. It's human nature to strive for better. But we have to allow for slip-ups and mistakes or we'll stop ourselves from living. Perfection is a myth. It's the mirage that keeps you struggling through. It doesn't exist. In order to build a more sustainable world, we need all of us trying to make changes incrementally, without the fear of making mistakes. A small number of people leading perfectly sustainable lives will get us nowhere; we have to act imperfectly all together.

14

Mental Decluttering

Decluttering is one method presented as a path to a more peaceful life, but the clear-out shouldn't stop at our physical spaces. In fact, it is an important part of any decluttering journey to pay attention to the state of our minds as well as that of our cupboards. By paying attention to our mental state we can allow ourselves the possibility of creating lasting change in our lives. This is a vast issue on which much has been written, but I will share what I have learned and found helpful. Writing about this is tricky, because if someone is really struggling, there's very little I can say that will help. The only wisdom that truly sticks is the wisdom we discover by ourselves, through experience and ageing. Reading, much as it can shape your ideas, can only effect internal change if it is accompanied by properly supported emotional work. From my own experience and my years of reading other mental health stories, nothing is truer than the saying 'No one can save you but yourself.' Yet I shall endeavour to offer a few thoughts on how to ease the mental pressures we all experience. This chapter will explore my own experiences with managing my mental health and offer some tools that I have found useful to help manage energy, time and headspace. But first, let's look at how we can look after ourselves after a decluttering process has been completed.

Post-decluttering self-care

Decluttering is an emotional process. After all unwanted physical items are removed from a home, it's really important to check in with yourself. Any feelings of guilt or grief for items now gone need to be processed fully and with self-compassion. I find journalling to be the most effective way of processing thoughts and emotions, but that isn't the case for everyone. Maybe choose a trusted friend to whom you can vent your feelings, if you prefer talking to writing. A technique that I have found to be beneficial for processing confusing emotions is proprioceptive writing. This process allows specific issues to be explored deeply through a structured journalling practice. You journal for twenty-five minutes at a time and use the question 'What do I mean by . . .?' to interrogate ideas that come up as you write. For example, if I write, 'I feel tired', asking 'What do I mean by *tired*?' can open up how you're actually feeling. It's a great way to build trust in yourself and your own feelings. It's honestly like DIY therapy. For more info, go to pwriting.org

I would also advise a post-clutter brain dump. By this, I mean write out all the to-do items swirling around in your head. Everything from 'learn Portuguese' to 'wash the dog' should be written down here. Then this list can be decluttered. Choose projects and aims that are truly important and achievable. Divide these items into long-term projects and short-term projects, house projects and personal projects – whatever categories work for you. This will hopefully help clear your head. Lists do not work for everyone, however, and no one understands more than me how unruly the insides of our minds can become.

Decluttering is a mammoth task, and it is important to reward yourself once a process is completed. If nothing else, this is positive reinforcement for future decluttering pushes. (Remember: it happens in layers.) Use the fancy bath salts you have been saving for good, read the book you forgot you owned, wear your most treasured garment, light the expensive candles. Enjoy your home and the work you've put into it. Savour the achievement.

My mental messiness

I am in an almost constant state of mental decluttering. My sensitive nature requires me to process everything that happens to me slowly and with attention. This is not always possible and can lead to what I call the 'emotional fatberg':[12] emotions pent up, unprocessed and causing a blockage in my mind which inevitably leads to system breakdown. My daily goal is to avoid the build-up of the fatberg. Writer Elizabeth Gilbert, of *Eat Pray Love* fame, talks about how writing is her hobby and her way of making a living, but her full-time job is looking after her mental health. So it is with me.

By my mid-twenties, it was clear that something had to give with my mental health. Pottering wasn't really cutting it in terms of managing my unruly emotions and each depression became worse than the last, even though by twenty-six I was on a heavy dose of SSRI antidepressants. After seven years of bouncing between different psychiatrists and therapists, I was lucky enough to find someone to whom I could speak honestly. This therapist encouraged me to come off all my numbing medication, a process which was extremely difficult and painful, but which allowed me to take responsibility for the emotions I was suppressing. After a gruelling six months of withdrawal from medication, I felt shaky and exhausted but empowered. I turned my focus from psychiatry to psychotherapy and I now take a low dose of SSRIs prescribed by my GP. Suppressing my emotions is no longer something I do and, while it's exhausting and difficult, I find it better than the numbness I experienced on medication. This issue is so personal, and I would never advise anyone to take or not take medication; what's right for me may not be right for you. If you are struggling, I hope so much that you can get the help you need, as I have been able to.

Mental health is a slippery little fish to write about. I have read many, many accounts over the years of people's struggles with their minds, and there is so much wisdom and courage to be found in those memoirs. There is, however, often an irritating conclusion to the stories. The person who has endured so much has pulled themselves out of the mire and is now flourishing. The messiness in their minds is now locked away in a drawer marked 'The

Past' and does not need to be revisited. Like a neatly ordered wardrobe frozen in a perfectly lit picture on Instagram, that part of their lives is folded, colour-coded, dealt with for ever.

I thought I had reached this state of being *finished* several times. Once I was medication-free and had taken back control of my own health, I felt invincible. Although I was warned that I would almost certainly get depressed again, I felt sure that I could handle it with my new lifestyle of exercise, therapy and self-awareness. A year or two later I was working in a job that appeared interesting but which I hated. It was in a loud office where there was constant talking, and I wasn't able for it, something I didn't fully realize at the time. I felt the usual mixture of shame, 'wrongness' and complete overwhelm. It was autumn, and the dark mornings were starting to take their toll.

Realizing that you are depressed again feels like thinking your house is clean and then moving the rug to find a hive of filthy scuttling insects. You realize they were always there and you are terrified that now they will never leave. As the weeks wore on and the nights got longer, I was coping by retreating to an unused meeting room, where I would sob and try to breathe. I would then return to my desk and laugh along with whatever was being laughed at with my colleagues. I was still living with my parents and, one evening, wishing to protect my family from how bad I was feeling, I stopped by a local park, lay down in some dark wet leaves and cried until my face hurt. The shame I felt for feeling bad again was vicious. I truly believed that it was all my fault.

I dragged myself through the holiday period and realized, with the encouragement of my family, that I might need to try medication again. This was, quite literally, a hard pill to swallow. I'd marked the 'Medication' chapter of my life as finished; I'd escaped the clutches of pharmacology and had emerged as an advocate for medication being used only as a last resort. But my life had unravelled again, and no amount of exercise and journalling and meditation was keeping me afloat. My only consolation was that, this time, it was my own choice to take the tablets. I wasn't blindly gobbling more and more of whatever the doctors gave me. I was in charge. I now take my medication free of shame and understand more fully how essential SSRIs and other drugs can be for people suffering from mental distress. There may be a time in the future when I need more medication again; I do not eliminate that option. It's an ongoing process, this task of mind-management. The stigma surrounding medication and mental health has been weakening by the day in this country, and I can only hope that positive change continues.

My mind is still a mess. Only yesterday I woke up riddled with fear and self-loathing, my confidence that I could write this book at zero and my future prospects looking fuzzy and bleak. One thing I do know by now is whether to fight it or whether to just sit and ride it out, like a shame head-cold. I cried, wrote in my journal, called Danny and cried some more. Then I made Bolognese and we watched *The Sopranos* and listened to The Sugarhill Gang, and I remembered that I've always wanted to learn the lyrics to 'Rapper's Delight' and I laughed. I woke up in tears this morning, having dreamt of a file of papers flying out of my reach, never to be retrieved. A mess. My mind is an uncleanable cupboard, liable to burst and spill its contents at any moment. Writing this a day later, I see that it isn't my fault. I have been blessed/cursed with a chaotic mind and a sensitive disposition. My life will always be messy – always. My task is to learn how to relax into the mess.

Burn-out

I'm sure most of us wish we could relax more. We live in a world that is bombarding us from every side – news reports, work emails, Whatsapp groups, promotional emails, social media notifications. It's no wonder there's currently an epidemic of mental burn-out. Modern work culture is characterized by the pressures of self-optimization, perfectionism and 24/7 contactability. This takes a huge mental toll on workers, with many people struggling to keep up whilst maintaining their health.

Burn-out is what happens when a person has been running on empty for too long with no rest. Symptoms include irritability, difficulty concentrating, lack of motivation and satisfaction, and physical complaints like sleep disturbance and digestive trouble. It is such a common phenomenon that in June 2019 the World Health Organisation announced it was recognizing burn-out as a medical condition for the first time. Unfortunately, the next day it emerged that they had changed their minds. As Oliver Burkeman commented in the *Guardian*: 'Let's be fair to the WHO staff, though; they're probably just very tired.'

The hope that technology would make life easier and give us more free time has long since been dispelled. We are living in notification hell. Did you know it can take up to thirty seconds for your body and mind to recover from the jolt of receiving a text or a new email? How often do you take those thirty seconds to process the shock of a new message? We are now contactable 24/7 and I, for one, can't cope! I frequently try to delete my social apps and request only essential contact from friends and family, only to cave in soon after and reinstall everything. I work freelance, which allows me flexibility, but it also means that if an email comes through late at night I feel that I have to respond because the buck stops with me. Let me offer a few key suggestions which have really helped me to manage my relationship with technology:

- Turn off notification sounds and icons on your phone. This allows you to check your messages when you want to, as opposed to when it is demanded of you. You soon realize that you don't have to reply immediately.
- Unsubscribe from unwanted emails such as brand newsletters when they arrive in your inbox. This takes a little time and can be irritating, but over time your inbox will contain only the essentials of your business and life.
- Don't have your phone in your bedroom. This is great advice, but I fall off the wagon all the time.

We are so wedded to our phones these days, they are like an extra limb! As a first step, you could leave it on a shelf or table across the room from your bed at night and then gradually wean yourself off checking it last thing at night and first thing in the morning.

- Unfollow or mute people or pages on social media that you are not interested in. This has been such a liberating habit to form and really eases the visual clutter of social media.
- Set timers on your social media use with apps such as OffTime or StayOnTask.
- Go through your online documents and delete any you no longer need. I found this process liberating but emotional. I came across many old job applications I had sent as a struggling twenty-something, which brought up unhappy memories. I know I'm a broken record by now, but please remember to be gentle with yourself, with this and any decluttering process.
- My favourite book about how to cope with the fast-paced demands of modern life is my good friend Aoife McElwain's *Slow at Work*. I genuinely keep it on my desk and refer to my favourite passages in times of need. Aoife writes with honesty and humour about her own experience of work-related burn-out and stress, and you might find it useful too.

Self-care

The word 'self-care' very much sums up the zeitgeist. We are told by the media, our bosses and our peers to look after ourselves, to take time out and learn how to manage our stress as part of a healthy lifestyle. As expected, the concept of self-care is now used to sell everything from luxury holidays to adult colouring books. What's not often noted is that the best self-care would probably come from a slowed-down work culture, with flexible working hours for parents and boundaries around contactability. But that idea requires collective action across industries, so it's easier to just give people a subscription to a meditation app.

Ronald Purser has written an eye-opening book about the sinister side of mindfulness meditation called *McMindfulness: How Mindfulness became the New Capitalist Spirituality.* He argues that mindfulness culture sends the message that an individual's mental well-being is entirely their own responsibility, not shared by their employer or the culture at large. This maintains the status quo and leaves burnt-out workers feeling that it's their own fault they can't keep up. It is the same idea of lumping the responsibility to recycle our way out of the environmental crisis on the consumer while the biggest polluters operate business-as-usual.

Self-care can often blend into self-optimization; it can feel like more work. I frequently feel that I *should* do more yoga, I *should* be mindfully meditating, I *should* buy an expensive Korean face mask. Often what I really need to do is *absolutely nothing.* My favourite chapter in *Slow at Work* concerns the recovery time we all need in order to perform at our best. This is a non-negotiable part of my life, and deviating from my routine of plenty of downtime between highly stimulating events has dire consequences for my mental state. Real self-care means understanding what our limits are and only operating within those boundaries. This is very much easier said than done, especially if you work in an environment which is hostile to employee well-being.

Knowing your limits

One of the most significant lessons I've learned about myself is how I process sensory input. This has been a crucial breakthrough and has helped me feel far less crazy, as well as allowing me to build a life which facilitates my temperament and protects my mental health. I was a very sensitive child and, as an adult, I continue to experience sensory stimulation and emotions very deeply. You could say I am an introvert, an empath, a highly sensitive person, or a selection of letters from the Myers Briggs personality scale. None of these fully explains what it's like to live inside my head.

It was never explained to me that I might process the world in a different way to my friends, siblings and cousins, so I grew up believing there was something wrong with me. I couldn't stay up as late as other people, I got tired more easily, I was more emotional. My energy has a very tight budget and if I fall into the red, I suffer the consequences, which include headaches, fatigue, digestive problems and depression.

On a physical level, I process sensory input differently to my more extrovert friends. I love going to festivals and parties, but if I stay somewhere noisy or high energy too long, the experience becomes seriously uncomfortable. The sensation is almost like a thermostat switch which flicks in my brain and I start to feel immediately uneasy and sometimes unwell. A sensory Cinderella, except that if I don't leave at midnight/ when I've had enough, it's me who turns into a weepy, exhausted pumpkin, not the carriage.

This is a tendency that I still frequently have to explain in my adult life, even as I get better and better at coping with my frustrating temperament. The sighs of disappointment from my friends when I want to leave an event early or take a walk by myself during a weekend away are part of the fabric of my life. Don't get me wrong, I have very kind and understanding friends. The thing is that my temperament is, well, hard to understand. If I say I'm introverted, people say, 'But you're not shy!', which is very true. If I say I'm 'highly sensitive', a term coined by psychologist Elaine Aron, people think I mean that I'm touchy, which isn't the full story. If I look back across the years of my mental health recovery, discovering Aron's book, *The Highly Sensitive Person*, was definitely a turning point. Reading it felt like reading my own biography. To learn that the way I experience the world is not unusual and is in fact totally understandable was a huge relief.

What I learned from Aron was that I experience sensory input such as noise and talking in a very deep way. This means that my tolerance for it is quite low and I need frequent recovery time to restore my energy and equilibrium.

To put it plainly, I get my energy from being by myself; being with other people, even though I'm not shy and am very sociable, is tiring and wears me down. My extrovert friends *need* stimulation and contact as this is how *their* energy is generated.

Being highly sensitive also means that I have a tendency to over-analyse and overthink things. This can lead to a mass of anxious and spiralling thoughts which can be difficult to silence. This headspace feels pretty cluttered, if you'll pardon the obvious metaphor. Sometimes people say, in an attempt to ease my woes, 'You're thinking about it all way too much!' I'm afraid asking someone with this temperament to change how they think is like telling a person with asthma to 'just try breathing better!' I understand my temperament now and have many tools to manage it, but if someone had told me when I was eleven or twelve that different people experience sensory stimulation in different ways, they would have saved me literally years of anguish. Understanding how our personal energy is generated is one of the key lessons of growing up. If your energy is out of whack, try and take some time to assess ways of changing your everyday routine to better suit your temperament. The key is managing your energy, not your time. The best way to start is to learn how to say a tiny but crucial word: no.

Saying no

In a world where busyness and stress are badges of honour, gaining control over our cluttered calendars can be a real struggle – particularly if you suffer from an affliction which plagued me in my twenties: people-pleasing. My symptoms included running errands for people I didn't even really like or care about, maintaining friendships I didn't want out of embarrassment, and saying yes to work I didn't want to do out of obligation. It was bloody exhausting.

We have to learn to prioritize our own comfort and health over other people's expectations of us. Now I fully embrace the Joy of Missing Out (JOMO) and am known to clap my hands with glee when plans are cancelled. Think back to my advice about keeping some storage space empty – just because you have the time, it doesn't mean you have to fill it. At the risk of sounding a bit like Oprah, you can't help anyone else if you yourself aren't well. If your people-pleasing tendencies are seriously affecting your quality of life, then I would gently suggest considering professional help.

Different strokes

If I had a dime for every time I've been given irritating and unsolicited mental health advice, I'd have . . . a lot of dimes. A fellow depressive friend and I often laugh about the well-meaning but patronizing 'Have you tried mindfulness?' comments we've received over the years. The path to reaching a place of relative mental well-being will look different for every single one of us. We all have to paddle our own canoes in this, and wrong turns can be taken.

When I was coming off all my medication, I was desperate for something to ease the overwhelming emotions I was experiencing. I decided that I needed to hide myself away from the world in order to 'find myself'. Most people go to Bali; I went to my childhood bedroom. I diligently practised mindfulness, like the good girl that I was. I obsessively read books on subjects like selfhood and emotional intelligence. I did yoga. I kept a daily gratitude diary, which made me feel horrendous because, on paper, my life looked great, but I was, in my self-critical mind, too ungrateful to be happy. I've never felt so lonely. After a few excruciating weeks of this, my therapist casually told me, 'Oh, mindfulness is actually very dangerous for someone who's badly depressed.' I would have screamed, but I was too exhausted. I have since learned that yes, for some people, mindfulness can make symptoms worse. A good book on this subject is *The Buddha Pill* by Miguel Farias and Catherine Wikholm. Again, what was wrong for me might be right for you. We are each unique in what we need to keep us balanced, and I do not mention this to put people off meditation. In fact, I now practise daily transcendental meditation, and it has proven helpful. I tell this story to illustrate what a long and winding road it can be to feel okay, and that dead ends and relapses are part of the process. And I have (more or less) made my peace with that.

Exercise, meditation, good sleep and a balanced diet are all obvious ways that we can improve our mental states. My routine now involves journalling, meditation, plenty of quiet, walking and a gentle stretching routine which I do myself at home. The most important thing I've learned is to give myself the space to feel bad if I need to.

A resource I love and use regularly is emmapb.com, the

website of psychotherapist Emma Philbin Bowman. In one of her many beautiful essays she explains that often those who are depressed are actually quite bad at feeling bad. Learning how to be with your negative moods and emotions without seeking to immediately wipe them out is an essential skill that we should all learn. That can be hard to understand in a world where 'positive thinking' is presented as a sure-fire way to feel permanently happy. The word 'happy' makes me cringe a little, to be honest. Yes, we are wired to strive for a peaceful and contented life and we cannot escape that urge. But often the effort to try to feel 100 per cent happy all of the time is the thing which makes us miserable. Remember: you are good enough just as you are, and you can change if you want to. Living contentedly amidst the mess of emotions thrown up at me from all angles is my everyday goal. May it be yours too.

Conclusion

We are nearing the end of our clutter journey. I hope this chapter has allowed you to slow down a little and to check in with how you're feeling. Mental health is talked about so much these days, but I'm not sure we've got quite there in terms of educating people on how to look after themselves *before* a crisis hits. The pace of modern life leaves so little time, if any at all, for us just to be with ourselves and to keep our internal life healthy. Self-compassion is such a necessary element of every person's life, and it's a tool we should be taught as children. But I know all too well how easy it is to read this and how hard it is to actually internalize this message.

This section has been about long-term change, from how we shop, to how we dispose of stuff, to how we manage stress. I never wanted to write a book about tidying your house, I wanted to write one that would sow seeds for long-term change. I hope there is something in this chapter for everyone, and I hope that small changes may blossom in your life that will steer you towards a more sustainable, connected and mentally healthy future.

Conclusion

Active Hope

There's a yoga bolster propping up my back on a deep chair. The table beside me holds a box of tissues and, although I'm crying, I don't use them. My therapist sits opposite me, calm as ever, waiting for me to speak. 'When will it be over?' I sob. 'When will I be finished?' My mind feels like a video game. I'm constantly zapping obstacles and getting to the next level, but I want to get to the end. 'Please.' My therapist looks at me and says, 'There is no end point. This is you now, fully alive and feeling everything deeply, like you always have.'

After some more crying, I leave her office and walk back to my car. I'm shaken. I am unfixable. My feelings and emotions can't all be neatly folded and tidied away. I have filed and organized my possessions, but I cannot, not now or ever, declutter the thoughts in my head.

There's a new blossom tree at the end of the road. It's so beautiful I stop and smell the white petals. I've known for a while that there's no end point, there's no game over. The same patterns, the same old sadnesses, come back again and again. It's how we respond to them that matters. That's the progress to strive for. No neatness, no solving. Just acceptance of the messiness of our lives.

The climate emergency we are facing is overwhelming. It is very difficult to know what we can do to help. What is clear is that pursuing infinite growth on a planet with finite resources simply does not add up. We have been operating as a multi-generational pyramid scheme, where the lives of future generations have been sacrificed for profit and convenience in the short term. Many people seem to think, 'Ah, sure, I'll be gone before it gets too bad.' But surely the Covid-19 crisis has shown us the very real and present consequences which can arise from not respecting the natural world. This is not a problem of the future, as I was taught in school, it is a problem for *now*.

A friend recently told me that she is often haunted by the thought of all the waste she has caused in her life and the amount she has consumed. She described how she has a vision of all these items and their packaging forming together into a giant waste-monster before her eyes. I felt sad that she was experiencing this shame and regret. We cannot get bogged down in thoughts of what might have been. A movement which I greatly admire is Active Hope, which gathers communities together to constructively work through environmental despair and harness energy for action over despondency. It was developed by ecologist Joanna Macy and Dr Chris Johnstone and has spread across the world. Active Hope uses small community groups to help build resilience and connection, which bolsters efforts to effect change.

It is often written that it is easier to imagine the end of the world than the end of capitalism. Having said that, I worked on this book during the Covid-19 crisis, which saw many governments around the world implement socialist responses to the disaster. We have seen how quickly things can change if the stakes are high enough. The economist David McWilliams wrote in May 2020 that 'Capitalism has been suspended.' I have seen so many thought pieces questioning a return to business-as-usual in favour of healthier and fairer working and living practices. Business writer Pilita Clark wrote in the *Financial Times* that 'my urge to splurge is over and won't be returning soon'. We shall have to wait and see whether normal service resumes post-Covid-19, or whether humanity can take the opportunity to build a society that is more equal for everyone and more gentle for our planet.

There is lots to hope for. An Accenture report from April 2020 called 'How Covid-19 Will Permanently Change Consumer Behaviour' threw up very promising data. It found that consumers' attitudes, behaviours and purchasing habits are changing, and that many of these will continue post-pandemic. According to Accenture, during the lockdown many of us became more mindful of what we were buying. We strove to limit food waste, to shop more cost consciously and buy more sustainable products. There was also a recognizable growing love for supporting local businesses. Eighty per cent of respondents said they felt more connected to their communities, and 88 per cent expected those connections to stay post-virus. We can only hope that these positive changes grow roots and become the norm.

Climate emergency is a vast and complicated problem, and that means the answer is complicated too. We need to drastically change our individual habits, but also join together in our collective responsibility to hold the true culprits, such as the fossil-fuel companies, accountable. We can be inspired by the essential work of activists like Naomi Klein, Isra Hirsi, Xiuhtezcatl Martinez, Rebecca Solnit and Greta Thunberg. We can learn to make better choices. We can make a difference. I am constantly learning, and my hope sometimes falters, but I come back every time to two rules of thumb:

1. The worst thing you can do about the climate emergency is nothing.
2. Recycling is a great place to start but a terrible place to stop.

There is hope in the fact that younger generations are becoming more and more environmentally conscious, as well as valuing experiences over items as sources of happiness. In fact, it has been proven that experiences such as holidays, festivals and cultural outings provide more enduring happiness than buying new stuff. I believe that more and more of us are looking for a different way of living outside the consumption-driven rat race. It's not about destroying all your possessions. It's about learning to value what you own in a new way. It's not about owning or doing as little as possible, it's about owning and doing the right things.

We need slower work, slower life and slower stuff. The phrase 'Reduce, reuse, recycle' is often touted, but we have forgotten that the first two words are far more important than the final one. Green consumerism offers us 'eco' products to try and divert our dollars, but the main things we need to do are simply:

- Buy less
- Buy local
- Buy long-lasting

The tide is beginning to turn. But the majority of us need to be on the same page to effect any significant and lasting change. As Soetsu Yanagi writes, 'If society contains a few outstanding individuals but the mass of people is mediocre, society as a whole will not prosper.'

Ten steps to take us forward:

1. Declutter your home gently and thoroughly.
2. Forgive yourself past purchasing mistakes.
3. Practise mindful materialism. Pay close attention to your possessions. Learn to love what you own. It really is transformational.
4. Identify any areas in your life where a desire to self-optimize is causing you anxiety. Do your best to unravel the roots of this compulsion. Seek professional help if necessary.
5. Get out of the habit of thinking that bringing items to charity shops whilst constantly buying new things is an adequate solution. Break the cycle. It is so much more important to question why we keep making unnecessary and wasteful purchases.

6. Buy less and buy better. Shop mindfully and be careful of the traps of sales and special offers. Take pride in supporting smaller and more ethical producers.

7. Share possessions with friends and relatives and learn to repair and properly care for the things you own.

8. Learn to care about where your possessions go when your use for them has ended. Question your allegiance to the concept of a bin. You never throw something away, you throw it somewhere else.

9. Personal changes are great and necessary, but if you can, engage with campaigns to bring better practices to all parts of the global system. Vote for the world you want to see.

10. With joy and with active hope, have nothing in your house that you do not know to be useful or believe to be beautiful.

Acknowledgements

I've always loved reading book acknowledgements, even though they are largely lists of names I don't recognize. Writing this is therefore a surreal experience. I'm not sure how I got to be in this position, but I owe a huge debt of gratitude to the following people.

Patricia Deevy, my commissioning editor, for believing in the project since day one, for taking a chance on me and for shaping the book so expertly.

Orla King for her eagle-eyed editing, for coaxing unruly paragraphs into something that made sense, and for her enthusiasm for this project since the start. The book would not be a quarter as good without you. Thank you, Orla.

My amazing copy-editor Sarah Day, and everyone at Sandycove and Penguin Random House who was involved in the process of pushing this book out into the world. It has been an incredible experience and I am so grateful for all of you.

Dr Shaun Cole, my MA supervisor. Thank you for allowing me to write the thesis that laid the groundwork for this book.

Hilary Fannin for making me seem interesting to a commissioning editor before they'd even seen a word I'd written. My gratitude is indescribable.

Niamh McCann for making a beautiful and thought-provoking piece of theatre.

Brenda Malone for allowing me to plunder her wisdom.

All the people I've quoted in this book, thank you!

Elaine Fitzgerald for changing my life. I'd never be here without you, I'm sure of that.

Susan Gill for her compassionate wisdom, and for pointing me towards the Seamus Heaney piece.

Aoife McElwain for holding my hand during the initial scary pitching stage, and for giving me the job of a lifetime at the Sing Along Social.

Ross Dungan, my video-game editor.

To all my wonderful friends far and near. I hope you know how much you all mean to me.

To my clients, who have taught me so much. Thank you for trusting me.

My early readers and editors – thank you for reining in my hyperbolic tendencies and for making me sound smarter than I am. In particular Aislinn Lucheroni for being, simply, the best.

My second family, the Murphy Brownes. Thank you for your love and support now and always. I'm so proud to be part of your clan.

My Nan, Cathy O'Sullivan, for giving me the best start in life and for all her wisdom and love.

My Grandmother, Joan Costello, for her endless support, friendship, and love.

My sister Rachel for her unwavering belief in me, her wisdom, and her dark sense of humour in times of need.

My brother Jack for his kindness and friendship, and for making me laugh. Disease is the release.

My dad Michael, for teaching me how to write a proper

sentence (I hope I was up to standard), and my mum Joan for giving me a love of books and reading. Thank you both for loving and supporting me so fiercely all these years. I would simply never have got here without you. This book is for you.

The biggest thank you of all is due to the wonderful person who became my husband whilst this mad little book was being written: Danny Browne; first reader, thoughtful editor, tear-wiper, tea-maker, laughter-bringer, love of my life. I know it's the cliché of clichés, but I truly will never know how I got so lucky.

Thank you all so, so much xx

Notes

1 Saxbe, D., and Repetti, R., 'For Better or Worse? Coregulation of Couples' Cortisol Levels and Mood States', *Journal of Personality and Social Psychology,* 2010, 98 (1), pp. 92–103.

2 Lamott, Anne, Bird by Bird: *Some Instructions on Writing and Life* (Canongate, 2020)

3 https://www.nytimes.com/2019/01/03/well/mind/clutter-stress-procrastination-psychology.html

4 https://www.theguardian.com/lifeandstyle/2020/may/19/silly-billy-what-the-ikea-bookcase-tells-us-about-the-true-cost-of-fast-furniture

5 https://www.pnas.org/content/107/38/16489

6 https://www.researchgate.net/publication/227591677_Happiness_in_Behaviour_Genetics_Findings_and_Implications

7 https://scholar.princeton.edu/sites/default/files/kahneman/files/anomalies_dk_jlk_rht_1991.pdf

8 https://pubmed.ncbi.nlm.nih.gov/22868937/

9 https://www.sciencedirect.com/science/article/pii/S0163638317301613

10 https://www.yourfatfriend.com/home/2019/10/15/the-bizarre-and-racist-history-of-the-bmi

11 Moran, Caitlin, *How to be a Woman* (Random House, 2011)

12 Disgusting build-up of waste in a sewer. Google it, it's gross.

Further Reading

If you would like to read more on some of the topics I have covered, here is a selection of books and articles I would recommend:

Decluttering

Aarssen, Cassandra, *The Clutter Connection* (Mango Publishing, 2019)

Dauch, Carly, et al., 'The Influence of the Number of Toys in the Environment on Toddlers' Play': https://www.sciencedirect.com/science/article/pii/S0163638317301613

de Barra, Laura, *Gaff Goddess* (Transworld Ireland, 2020)

Dinh, Thuy, 'Marie Kondo's Advice for Decluttering Threatens the Cultural Heritage of Refugees Like Me': https://www.nbcnews.com/think/opinion/marie-kondo-s-advice-decluttering-threatens-cultural-heritage-refugees-me-ncna1012661

Emma, *The Mental Load, A Feminist Comic* (Seven Stories Press, 2018)

Harford, Tim, *Messy: How to be Resilient and Creative in a Tidy-minded World* (Little, Brown, 2016)

Lucchesi, Emilie Le Beau, 'The Unbearable Heaviness of Clutter': https://www.nytimes.com/2019/01/03/well/mind/clutter-stress-procrastination-psychology.html

Kahneman, Daniel, Knetsch, Jack L., and Thaler, Richard H., 'Anomalies: The Endowment Effect, Loss Aversion, and Status Quo Bias', *Journal of Economic Perspectives*, 5 (1), winter 1991, pp. 193–206: https://scholar.princeton.edu/sites/default/files/kahneman/files/anomalies_dk_jlk_rht_1991.pdf

Saxbe, D., and Repetti, R., 'For Better or Worse? Coregulation of Couples' Cortisol Levels and Mood States', *Journal of Personality and Social Psychology*, 2010, 98 (1), pp. 92–103

Shepherd, Marshall, 'The Science behind Why People Buy Bread When Snow is in the Forecast': https://www.forbes.com/sites/marshallshepherd/2017/01/06/the-science-of-why-people-buy-bread-when-snow-is-in-the-forecast/#2d735e52 5978

Tebbe, Jason, 'Twenty-first-century Victorians': https://www.jacobinmag.com/2016/10/victorian-values-fitness-organic-wealth-parenthood/

Tolin, David F., et al., 'Neural Mechanisms of Decision-making in Hoarding Disorder': https://pubmed.ncbi.nlm.nih.gov/228 68937/

Wiseman, Eva, 'Decluttering: A Load of Junk?': https://www.theguardian.com/books/2015/jun/14/decluttering-a-load-of-junk-the-life-changing-magic-of-tidying

Capitalism and Material Culture

Curtis, Adam, *The Century of the Self*, documentary film

Heaney, Seamus, 'The Sense of the Past': https://www.historyireland.com/20th-century-contemporary-history/the-sense-of-the-past-by-seamus-heaney/

Humphreys, Kim, *Excess: Anti-Consumerism in the West* (Polity, 2013)

Kahneman, Daniel, and Deaton, Angus, 'High Income Improves Evaluation of Life but not Emotional Well-being': https://www.pnas.org/content/107/38/16489

Klein, Naomi, *No Logo* (Flamingo, 2001)

Nes, Ragnhild Bang, 'Happiness in Behaviour Genetics: Findings and Implications': https://www.researchgate.net/publication/227591677_Happiness_in_Behaviour_Genetics_Findings_and_Implications

Oryema, Wilson, *Boxing Day Blues*, film (you can find it on Vimeo)

Schwartz, Barry, *The Paradox of Choice* (Harper Perennial, 2019)

Sennett, Richard, *The Craftsman* (Penguin, 2019)

Usborne, Simon, 'Silly Billy: What the Ikea Bookcase Tells Us about the True Cost of Fast Furniture': https://www.theguardian.com/lifeandstyle/2020/may/19/silly-billy-what-the-ikea-bookcase-tells-us-about-the-true-cost-of-fast-furniture

Yanagi, Soetsu, *The Beauty of Everyday Things* (Penguin, 2019)

Sustainability

Fletcher, Kate, *The Craft of Use* (Routledge, 2016)

Hoskins, Tansy, *Stitched Up* (Pluto Press, 2014)

Johnstone, Chris, and Macy, Joanna, *Active Hope: How to Face the Mess We're in Without Going Crazy* (New World Library, 2012)

Minney, Safia, *Slow Fashion* (New Internationalist, 2016)

Shine, Dr Tara, *How to Save Your Planet One Object at a Time* (Simon and Schuster, 2020)

Strasser, Susan, *Waste and Want: A Social History of Trash* (Henry Holt and Company, 1999)

Trentman, Frank, *The Empire of Things: How We Became a World of Consumers, from the Fifteenth Century to the Twenty-first* (Allen Lane, 2016)

Body Image and Wardrobes

Fannin, Hilary, 'My Mum's Diary Entry When She was 89: "Lose Weight Now!"': https://www.irishtimes.com/life-and-style/people/my-mum-s-diary-entry-when-she-was-89-lose-weight-now-1.3774811

Frances-White, Deborah, *The Guilty Feminist* (Hachette, 2018)

Guy, Ali, Green, Eileen, and Banim, Maura (eds), *Through the Wardrobe: Women's Relationships with Their Clothes* (Berg, 2011)

Harrison, Christy, *Anti-Diet* (Hachette, 2019)

Hustvedt, Siri, *The Blazing World* (Simon and Schuster, 2014)

Hustvedt, Siri, 'Outside the Mirror': https://www.independent.co.uk/arts-entertainment/books/features/siri-hustvedt-on-style-outside-the-mirror-7827274.html

Moran, Caitlin, *How to be a Woman* (Random House, 2011)

Nolan, Megan, 'Why Do We All Have to be Beautiful?': https://www.nytimes.com/2019/04/06/opinion/sunday/women-beauty.html

O'Connor, Annmarie, *The Happy Closet* (Gill, 2015)

Wolf, Naomi, *The Beauty Myth* (HarperCollins, 2009)

Mental Health

Aron, Elaine, H., *The Highly Sensitive Person* (HarperCollins, 2014)

Brown, Brené, *Daring Greatly* (Penguin, 2013)

Farias, Miguel and Wikholm, Catherine, *The Buddha Pill* (Watkins Publishing, 2015)

Gaffney, Maureen, *Flourishing* (Penguin Ireland, 2011)

Gilbert, Daniel, *Stumbling on Happiness* (HarperCollins, 2009)

Lamott, Anne, *Bird by Bird: Some Instructions on Writing and Life* (Canongate, 2020)

McElwain, Aoife, *Slow at Work* (Gill and Macmillan, 2017)

Purser, Ronald E., *McMindfulness: How Mindfulness became the New Capitalist Spirituality* (Watkins Media Ltd, 2019)

Simmons, Rachel, *The Curse of the Good Girl* (Penguin, 2009)

Trichter Metcalf, Linda, and Simon, Tobin, *Writing the Mind Alive: The Proprioceptive Method for Finding Your Authentic Voice* (Random House, 2008)